The Dialogue Gap

THOMAS J. MULLEN

ABINGDON PRESS ⓐ nashville and new york

THE DIALOGUE GAP

Copyright © 1969 by Abingdon Press

Standard Book Number: 687-10722-9

Library of Congress Catalog Card Number: 69-18444

SET UP, PRINTED, AND BOUND BY THE
PARTHENON PRESS, AT NASHVILLE,
TENNESSEE, UNITED STATES OF AMERICA

preface

The gap between radical Christians and conservative ones is large, and it is growing. Having recently joined the faculty of a Christian college and become connected with a new seminary after ten years in the parish ministry, I have witnessed misunderstanding and confusion between Christians demonstrated again and again. Nearly every denomination faces the problem of a religious dialogue gap, with the Body of Christ not really knowing (much less trusting) what its left and right hands are doing.

In a world and a country torn by social unrest, the shaking of the foundations, and the hungry reaching of people for meaning in their lives, the Church of Jesus Christ cannot afford the internal division which now exists—especially at the local level. Persons who have been faithful members of congregations all their lives are dropping out. Young seminarians are saying they cannot serve a local church in good conscience. Ministers are being fired for disturbing the *status quo,* and others are resigning because they aren't able to disturb the *status quo.*

This book is an attempt to promote dialogue among the very Christians who are most at odds with each other. It is written deliberately as a study book, and the final four chapters conclude with questions, cases, real-life situations which invite solutions, and statements which deserve to be challenged or endorsed. In this sense, it is an open-ended book, one which we hope will inspire the reading of other books and considerable discussion in local churches. The questions and problems raised are not hypothetical; they come out of the experience of many group meetings (some rather heated), and are raised primarily by participants. Clearly, you, the reader, will want to add to the questions, or you may even want to sponsor a book burning after church some Sunday. This is perfectly satisfactory to both the author and Abingdon Press, so long as the books are paid for in advance. More important, however, is the necessity of setting our minds and our emotions to the serious task of narrowing the dialogue gap which is an albatross of evil about the neck of the church.

Special appreciation is due Doris Burkhart, my perceptive secretary, who has managed both to read my writing and keep her patience at the same time. My wife Nancy served as chief critic for the manuscript, and most of the faults of the book are her responsibility, as she is more sensitive to her husband's human needs than his literary weaknesses—for which this author thanks God.

TOM MULLEN

contents

chapter one

A NEW BREED OF CHRISTIAN

There is a new breed of Christian abroad in the land. He may come from a traditional church, and he may have been nursed at the breast of orthodox, middle-class piety, but he is not the product which the local church expected and certainly not that which was intended.

The average man in an average church with an average understanding of Christianity is baffled by the new breed of Christian. He may even be disturbed or angered by what he sees and hears *in the name of his church* today. He undoubtedly wonders, at times, what in the world some of it has to do with the Bible or theology or even ordinary common decency.

As Mr. Average Christian looks about him, he sees that timid pastors have come down from their pulpits to march with Negroes in acts of civil disobedience. He may pick up his newspaper and read about a Baptist minister in Rochester, New York, who, along with other ministers, led the effort to raise a hundred thousand dollars to finance a two-year FIGHT campaign against racial injustice. Even more disturbing, probably, is the news that the money was used to hire labor-style organizers to bring pressure on landlords and city officials.

Episcopalians are probably no less shocked to learn that one of their priests runs, along with some other Protestants and a Franciscan Friar (of all people!), a school for high school dropouts. When school is out, he and his compatriots involve themselves in rough and tumble political campaigns, fighting hard *against* tax hikes or *for* them, as the occasion demands. Many mainline Christians would be even more shocked if they could experience a weekend at Chicago's Ecumenical Institute wherein seventeen young families operate a new religious community out on the city's crummy and slummy west side. They might even cry "communism" when they discover that the Institute is a contemporary version of the communal Christian sects which existed when America was young.

Clearly, this new breed of Christian does not represent the majority of church members, but equally clear is the fact that they represent a significant—and growing—number of persons who have taken religion out of the cloister and into the street. Ministers run for public office and do so *explicitly* as part of their Christian witness. Clergy and other Christians organize to oppose the war in Vietnam, sometimes dropping out of their leadership roles in the local church to do so.

Laymen refuse to attend meetings of the men's club at St. John's on the Corner, but they freely give of their time and energy in government-sponsored poverty programs, in the name, once again, of their Christian faith.

The new breed does not limit itself, however, simply to adventures in the realm of Christian social action. Its statements, its attitudes, and its practices in the area of personal morality are often more unsettling to the established church than what is done and said in behalf of civil rights, the war on poverty, or the minimum wage. After all, there have always been outspoken pacifists, radical Christian activists, and militant crusaders. However, some among the new breed of Christian seem to be upsetting what has been accepted Christian morality for centuries.

Not long ago, in England, the Rev. Harry Williams, Dean of Trinity College, made the startling statement that premarital or extramarital intercourse might be not only permissible but also "a healing asset where Christ was present." Other men and women, both clergy and laity, in the name of their Christianity, may work to bring about a change in laws prohibiting abortion. Or they may come out in favor of euthanasia (mercy killing) under certain circumstances, a question that bewilders doctors, and which the church has traditionally opposed for centuries. Recent public statements by clergymen and some Christian doctors and attorneys favored more understanding treatment for homosexuals and petitioned for court action that would keep publishers of certain kinds of erotic literature out of jail. College chaplains have been known to advocate that infirmaries dispense birth control pills to unmarried collegians, and theologians write articles for *Playboy* and other magazines which ten years ago they wouldn't have had the nerve to buy from a newsstand.

As if a revolution in social action and personal morality were not enough, the past few years have seen a revolution in theology. The radical idea of the "death of God" immediately captured a wide audience, and just as quickly alienated thousands of orthodox Christians, who wondered what in the name of God (if there were one) was going on. Even though this kind of radical theology made little impact on the seminaries, it did indicate the earnest questioning of *basic* Christian ideas that heretofore had been taken for granted. Many young Christians revealed that they were ready to abandon the word "God" because they felt that churchgoing millions merely used it as a nickname for a superstition that really meant nothing to them.

Hundreds of prayer groups are springing up *outside* the churches, and in many large and small cities sectlike groups of "Christian bohemians" exist which have no formal connection with an established denomination or local church. In other words, for perhaps the first time in history the existence and reality of God and the importance of the church are being questioned by persons who think of themselves as Christian but who are outside the institution. Even more significant is the fact that the spokesmen for the new, questioning theologies are not merely innovators. They are also reflectors of genuine theological unrest. In fact, the radical theologians regard themselves as realists, who cut through the tangle of today's world to confront the secular nature of our society as it is and speak about

14

it and to it on a level that secular man can hear. Therefore, many contemporary Christians are saying good-
bye to such traditional beliefs as the Trinity, the
virgin birth, or even the incarnation. Most of the new
breed do not openly deny their belief in these fundamentals, but many among them agree that these orthodoxies are simply not worth fussing about today.

It needs to be made clear that the "new breed" is
not a term which applies only to theologically trained
ministers and a few college professors. The young adult
—certainly the college student—is rejecting, or has already rejected, what he calls provincialism, piety, and
sentimentality. Much to the chagrin of parents and
grandparents, the new breed doesn't like the local
church very much. At least, he doesn't like it as it is
now constituted. He may attend occasionally to please
his parents or to meet social expectations, but when
he is back at his college or taking his coffee break with
other junior executives, he confesses his boredom,
laughs at the church's absurdities, and ridicules the
minister. It can even be said that this kind of Christian
hates the church in the sense that he is much more
impatient than many of his predecessors with the whole
institutional apparatus. He regards the organizational
structures of Christian bodies as obstacles to the "real"
work of the church.

That this attitude can be excused as mere sophomoric
sour grapes is a possibility, but not all of these contemporary Christians are young—at least in body.
Again and again, we find mature Christians criticizing
the church for its irrelevance, its busybodyness, and its
hypocrisy. Clearly, these criticisms represent their *considered* opinion. This is why a high school teacher of

several years of experience decides that he wants to go to a mission field or serve in a social agency, partly because, as he put it, "American Christians are trapped by their own affluence."

The local churches, and certainly so-called Christian America, are part of the problem, not part of the answer, in the minds of many among the new breed. A college teacher of religion drops out of his local Baptist church because the whole institution, he says, seems to function as the "custodian of the *status quo*." A middle-aged housewife sticks with her church because of commitments to the family and her friends, but privately she expresses radical disagreement with its theology, its moralistic attitude, and the way it spends time and money. We must conclude, in other words, that if radical thinkers and leaders seem to represent the clergy and the university community only, we must also add that by this time there are many others from many walks of life who can be included among the new breed as a result of their own restlessness and their *acceptance* of these radical ideas.

Indeed, if there is a single common characteristic of the new breed, it is the mood of criticism which permeates their ranks. There have, of course, always been prophetic voices among Christians, but generally the mood of the Christian in the churches was that of acceptance and conformity. In the years since World War II, at least, the word "Christian" would have described a kind of pleasant, friendly citizen who represented virtuous, middle-class America. "Christian" meant that a person was "good," i.e., well behaved, respectable, honest, and diligent in church attendance. You will recall that it was during this time that church attendance soared to all-time highs, "under God" was restored to the Pledge of Allegiance, and Billy Graham was named America's outstanding religious figure several years in a row. It was during this time that Norman Vincent Peale's "peace-of-mind" books were selling like hot cakes, and the "prayer breakfast" became popular religio-political activity. The "good Christian" went to Sunday school, and his children attended MYF, FYF, BYF, or XYF, where they learned how to behave in a "Christian" manner on a date. Then everybody went out and played softball. The stereotype of a Christian was based upon a rural or suburban model, and even urban Christians were usually transplants from small towns or children of the Christian "folk" whose parents came from rural areas.

The critical attitude of the new breed begins with a rejection of this very stereotype which we have described. A whole flock of books has been produced in recent years which attacks the local church at this very point.[1] One of the most outspoken critics has been Archie Hargraves in his booklet on church renewal entitled, appropriately, "Stop Pussyfooting Through a Revolution." [2] His arguments are typical of the mood of criticism which the new breed demonstrates:

1. The Church worships a God but many times it is the false God of the *status quo*—the church as it is, the

[1] See, for example, Pierre Berton, *The Comfortable Pew;* William Stringfellow, *A Private and Public Faith;* Stephen Rose, *Who's Killing the Church;* Colin Williams, *Where in the World?;* and Gibson Winter, *The Suburban Captivity of the Churches.*

[2] The ideas expressed in the author's summary, ending on p. 19, are Hargraves' and are used by permission of the Stewardship Council of the United Church of Christ.

community as it is, and the world as it is. The local church, it is charged, won't change and, consequently, is unable to bring about changes in the society that surrounds it.

2. The church has entered a period Gibson Winter calls its "suburban captivity." Evidence for this criticism is the fact that residential churches have fled the deteriorated areas of the inner city and have become contemporary temples for the glorification of the middle class. Church members are accused of being more interested in architecture than the Gospel and in maintaining the edifice than in extending God's good news.

3. The church seeks to be popular although the Christian Gospel requires it to be unpopular in many instances. To be a Christian is to be respectable and well-received in the community, a far different meaning—say its critics—from that of the New Testament in which the word "parish" meant a "body of aliens in the midst of any community."

4. The church exists primarily for its own members instead of for the outside world. Congregations that quickly approve the purchase of an organ costing thousands of dollars may disagree for hours over whether or not some local community-action projects should be included. This introversion antagonizes the youth of today, who turn instead to the Peace Corps or Civil Rights activities.

5. Most members of most churches use their places of worship as they would a filling station—as places to which they go occasionally in order to refuel. The church, say many among the new breed, is the place where one learns only how to think positively and find "peace of mind."

6. Church members regard God as the "Great Psychia-

18

trist," a helpful resource to call upon in times of need and a worthy friend if a loved one dies but a convenient absentee at other times. The local church is thus accused of running a spiritual ambulance service, treating suffering when it arises but rarely trying to influence the power structure that might have caused the suffering in the first place.

7. The church as an agent of Christian education fails to nurture the spiritual growth of its members. Church membership means so little that some people can join by phone without even being physically present. When the Sunday morning service is over and past, for the vast majority of the members of that church, the reason for their membership is over for the week. Huge congregations may draw four to ten persons to Bible study or prayer groups, and many churches don't even bother to schedule such events at all.

8. The local church allows its life to be governed by traditions that are long out of date. Persons who suggest changing the time of worship from 11:00 A.M. to 10:30 A.M. encounter strong resistance, as the members of the church overlook the fact that the eleven o'clock hour was set up originally by an agrarian society to avoid conflicting with the time for milking cows.

This feeling of criticism is very real among the new breed. They know what they don't like, and what they don't like is much of what they see, or think they see, in the local church. While many of their number do not know quite what to put in the place of the local church and the other Christian institutions we now have, they are clear in their own minds that the practice of the Christian religion on the local level ranges between inefficiency at best to abomination before God at worst.

Not only is there a mood of criticism that characterizes the new breed, there is also an acceptance of secularism and "worldliness" that is peculiar to our time. The younger generation of Christians is a product of a time in history different from any past time. Many of them have never lived B.T.—before television. Many of them have been brought up in a world in which the public press assumes that most citizens will *not* be in or around a church on Sunday mornings. Practically all of them have been exposed to a greater variety of cultures, social practices, and ideas than their parents would have deemed possible.

Members of the young generation are persons who are part of the scientific age, and ever since they were in kindergarten, their teachers and their school systems have been telling them that man can solve his problems if he thinks about them long enough and works at the solutions hard enough. This writer could not help but notice the difference in the reaction of an Old Testament class he taught at Earlham College last year compared to the one he was a member of as a student fifteen years ago. Just fifteen years ago the teacher worried about disturbing the faith of the students who came to college, as students usually came believing literally in the Bible, accepting the stories of Noah, Jonah, and the rest at face value. Essentially, they were unfamiliar with higher criticisms of the Bible. Now, with many Sunday schools approaching the Bible critically themselves, and with many students having little confidence in the Bible as anything more than a collection of antiquated stories, the teacher must work to get his students to take the Bible seriously. There is no difficulty in getting students to approach the Bible critically; there is considerable challenge in encouraging them to regard it as somehow holy. For many there is little biblical knowledge to be challenged, and biblical illiteracy is normative.

The new breed has also been brought up in a world in which there is more governmental involvement in social causes than ever before. The church obviously is not the prime agent in dealing with human problems and misery. In fact, the conservative church many times seems to the new breed to stand in the way of such activities. In a sense we now live in a "sociologist's America," an America in which we expect to solve problems first by taking a survey, secondly, by hiring a team of social workers; and finally, by distributing the results of their findings. The reaction of the new breed, in short, is to respond *professionally* to human needs, and good deeds are better done when not taken on by amateurs.

In daily contacts, too, the new breed demonstrates a kind of acceptance and tolerance of nonpracticing Christians and non-Christian ideas that is different from the days of their parents. Many of the close friends and acquaintances of the new breed are themselves thoroughly secularized, and would disavow any connection with a Christian church. Today's young Christian finds it very difficult indeed to think in terms of a religion that excludes these friends whom he knows intimately and personally; and one of the reasons few ministers preach about hell anymore is because so many adults have so many friends who are, in the preacher's terms, candidates for it! The mood of tolerance is heightened by the fact that American decency and good-guy attributes are well known, and if a non-Christian demonstrates these qualities, then surely the world can't be so bad or so "lost" after all. At college the young Christian may have been confronted by fellow students with very different backgrounds from his own, and if he does not agree with his roommate's conclusions about sex and abortion and free love, he is still more acceptant of the persons who hold those ideas than his parents or grandparents would like for him to be.

Thus, when radical theologians suggest that we must have a secular kind of Christianity, the young Christian will eagerly respond. The language of this appeal is familiar because his way of life has been a constant bombardment since childhood of secular ideas, promoted by teachers he personally respects and held by persons he personally likes. For the new breed, in fact, the word "secular" is not a "bad" word at all, and sermons attacking secularism will fall on unheeding ears.

If the established church smarts from new-breed attacks on traditional structures and long-standing practices, it becomes positively angry when it sees the strange bedfellows these outspoken Christians choose. Unsavory politicians, left-wing organizations, and cultists of one kind or another seem at times to be prime allies in word and deed with the new breed. Racial demonstrations often involve atheistic beatniks, and Christian pacifists may march with young socialists for freedom. An avowed atheist, such as Bertrand Russell, may oppose the war in Vietnam—along with the president of the National Council of Churches. Hugh Hefner may work side by side with an Episcopal priest to fight censorship, albeit for different reasons.

Young Christians who are more sure of what they

are against than what they favor may worry less about their fellow crusaders than do orthodox members of the church establishment, and so they stand exposed to criticism which marks guilt by association. One young student, a member of a local church I served, participated in a peace march in Washington and later wrote a letter appealing for understanding. She was concerned lest her friends and parents believe the news stories which implied that the demonstration had been controlled by communists. One comment in her letter was particularly significant: "There are no communists here to speak of, but *even if there were, this cause is right!*" (Italics mine.)

In short, not only is there a generation gap between many of the new breed and the local church, there is also a "tolerance gap." The new breed is not so concerned about who their bedfellows are, so long as their cause is right. Indeed, it is difficult to define who the new breed are at times, precisely because there is such a diversity of belief and motivation within the groups with which they identify. A bright young pagan may seek an open-dormitory policy at his college because he likes to sleep with girls; but a concerned and responsible young adult may be convinced, rightly or wrongly, that open dorms are the best way to learn sexual self-control. Twentieth-century rebels may enjoy demonstrating in the streets as a way of spitting in the face of white, Anglo-Saxon Protestants who seem to cramp his personal desires to do as he damn well pleases. A twentieth-century Christian may also demonstrate in the streets because he's become convinced that this is the only way he can call attention to his cry for justice.

23

The motives are diverse, and the mood of the new breed is to overlook the worrisome matter of who their bedfellows are. Today's young Christians are confident that they can pick and choose from among the philosophies available, and they are sure they have the ability to decide what is constructive and what is not. They feel sure the church has much to learn from the world, and they are unwilling to separate themselves from it. The key word is dialogue, not monologue, and the new breed regards itself as a movement of anguished young Christians who want desperately to learn for themselves the meaning of obedience in the *real* world at this time in history.

The surprising thing, however, is that the new breed is so naïve about the effect of their words and actions on the establishment. We should *expect* many Christians in the local church who represent a different perspective and a conservative point of view to be shocked by, and resentful of, what they see and hear, especially as reported in the popular press. For a middle-aged and conscientious Methodist to read that seminary professors are promoting the idea that God is dead, and then respond with indifference, would be astounding, and we really should expect nothing else than a negative reaction. While a large percentage of Americans— possibly more than half—is under thirty years of age, the percentage of persons over thirty (or even fifty) in a local church is dramatically higher. The natural conservatism of the local church is therefore appalled by these radical ideas, and it is no wonder that some otherwise tender people perceive a subtle communist plot to subvert the churches.

No wonder a reporter for a Baptist periodical returned in wrath from a worship conference of his denomination where, among other things, the attenders had been asked to listen to a jazz interpretation of scripture and to meditate on a passage of Norman Mailer's that cited Ernest Hemingway and Marilyn Monroe as models to follow. "If this is the wave of the future," he said, "the gates of hell need not quiver." Are we really surprised that Bishop Pike was tried for heresy? Given the radical questions he has been asking, how could he be confronted in any other way?

The writer of a letter to the editor of *The Christian Century* probably expressed the feelings of many orthodox Christians when he responded to Waldo Beach's review of *Living With Sex* by Richard F. Hettlinger.[3]

Mr. Beach states that the Bible "offers no help" on this topic. I . . . think I am on safe ground when I say that the Bible has done more to control illicit sex drives than any other force in society. Is the moral law contained in the Bible no factor? Is it not true that God wrote the moral law into the very constitution of this universe? It was true long, long before the Commandments were written.

Mr. Beach speaks of the "moral sensitivity" of Hettlinger. He then quotes the passage in the book that states that fornication between an engaged couple "will be little different in its significance for them, if it precedes marriage. . . . it need not be inconsistent with eventual marital success and happiness."

If this book is supposed to be a guide to the "bewildered" student, may God help the poor student! Seldom in the history of the church have we had more experts who are themselves "blind as bats" guiding youth to some of the

[3] *The Christian Century,* June 21, 1967, p. 816.

simplest moral principles clearly taught in the Bible. We are being disintegrated by that half-baked philosophy called "situational ethics." One of our Toronto newspapers had an article by a leading Toronto clergyman entitled "Adultery—Is It Always Wrong?" When the clergy start putting question marks after the moral law, then may God help us.

No wonder many concerned Christians wring their hands and ask, "What is the world coming to?" No wonder some Christians may leaf quickly through their Bibles to the book of Revelation, looking there for signs that we are in the latter days. Not surprising, either, is the fact that many responsible, "modern" ministers and progressive laymen have come to feel uneasy over the radical nature of this assortment of persons within the church we have loosely identified as the new breed. It is becoming harder and harder to tell the good guys from the bad guys.

This, it seems to the author, is the real tragedy. The new breed needs to be understood, but it also needs to understand the conservative church. The established, main-line churches run the risk of sweeping their own problems and their serious failures under the blanket of rejection with which they cover the "heresies" of the new breed. The fundamental problem is that of a "dialogue gap." Both camps have been making a common mistake: they have been turning each other off and tuning each other out. Both have made a basic error: They have forgotten that today's revolutions are tomorrow's orthodoxies.

Religion is in a period of great risk and danger, and those who look for certainty and security in the church are in for a rough time. The local church no longer can afford the luxury of simply being on the defensive. It has to listen to what the new breed is saying or it will very likely lose its growing edge and quietly fade away into a stained-glass sunset. The local church needs to face squarely the criticism which is directed toward it and accept the fact that some, much, or even all of it may be justified. It needs to be more selective in its rejection of radical ideas and radical proponents of ideas, choosing carefully on the basis of considered judgment and not in terms of angry frustration. It needs to listen with its hearing aid turned up so as to discern fairly whether it is God or man speaking.

Radical Christians share the responsibility for dialogue, too, and they have seemed at times to be throwing the baby out with the bath water. The local churches which gave birth to many of them are not as conservative as their moments of frustration would sometimes lead them to believe. The new breed needs to be as carefully critical of itself as it has been critical of the local church, for in the fantastic outpouring of ideas and practices which have come forth in the name of "Christian relevance," common sense assures us that truth and faddism are undoubtedly intertwined.

D. Elton Trueblood has warned us, too, of one special danger which must be taken seriously by twentieth-century seekers:

One of the reigning tenets of our time is the extreme belief that all our problems are new. I would call this, really, the disease of contemporaneity. Shall I give you an example? Last winter I was speaking to a group of pastors in a certain state, and I advised these men to study Augustine's

Confessions and the *Imitation of Christ* and Pascal's *Pensées,* and John Woolman's *Journal.* Right away one of the leading clergymen said, "Oh, those were all very well for another day. But so much has happened now that their appeal is utterly undermined. We are in a new world, and these books have nothing to say to our situation at this moment." . . . This means that we cut ourselves off from the wisdom of the ages, including that of the Bible. It means that, if this is taken seriously, we are really an orphan generation—an orphan generation that takes itself far too seriously, that is too much impressed with changes that may be only superficial. . . . Contemporaneity when it is a disease is a very damaging disease, because it destroys the continuity of culture.[4]

The new breed needs the perspective of history. One of its most serious dangers is its suspicion of tradition and its too-easy embrace of that which seems contemporary and, therefore, acceptable.

An unwillingness on the part of either the local church or its radical critics to dialogue with the other is arrogance that can only divide the church of Jesus Christ. A stereotyping of the new breed as wild-eyed heretics or pinkish radicals is no more helpful than the tendency of the new breed of Christians to cross off the local church as nothing more than the religious arm of the country club.

What must be taken seriously by both sides is that the church is undergoing a genuine, 100-proof revolution. Every couple of centuries, Christianity breaks out of its institutional boxes and builds fires—fires which

---

[4] "Ideas That Shape the American Mind." *Christianity Today,* January 6, 1967, p. 3. Copyright 1967 by *Christianity Today;* reprinted by permission.

provide both heat and light. The eruption almost always includes a shaking in the structures of organized religion and a confrontation between generations, ideologies, and methods. The sixteenth century's Reformation started Protestantism and undercut feudalism. The eighteenth century's Great Awakening extended the Gospel to the poor, roused them to seek education and a better life, and provided a vision which helped build America's mass middle class. Someday church historians will write of the twentieth century's "worldly Christianity" as a bona fide revolution, too, and it is important that we be aware of the dimensions of our current upheaval within the church.

Atheism—or what may be judged as such—may be more reverent than empty conformities, and anguish over faith, more genuine than purely formal acquiescence. This revolution, as is true with most revolutions, expresses God's judgment—judgment on a church that has turned in upon itself and, at times, forgotten that Christ died for the world and not for the church. At the same time, the new breed must see that while the secular city is a reality, it is not necessarily the New Jerusalem. Seeking for a new and fresh understanding of God in new and fresh ways is vital, but even now we must learn from the past, which created yesterday's radicals who are today's old fogies.

If an authentic dialogue can take place, the total church stands a good chance of discovering or, in some cases, rediscovering a firsthand experience of faith for itself. For out of turmoil comes rebirth, and out of controversy can come new truth. If the dialogue gap can be bridged, if we can go beyond our stereotypes and biases, if we can tune in what has been tuned out, and if we can be more generous with the label "Christian"—we may be able to share in the rare experience of discovering God's will for this time and this place. John A. T. Robinson, one of the catalytic agents in the present turmoil, has stated the problem forthrightly.

Can the Church work from both ends like this without breaking in the middle? Can its right hand respect, even when it does not know, what its left hand is doing? This will be the test of its unity in the period ahead of us. Division denominationally is not, I trust, likely to be the threat of the new Reformation. Division and disintegration within each denomination, each local church, and indeed each Christian, produced by the strain of living in the overlap is an all too present possibility. Can the Church survive it? My faith is that it can—just. And that is why I believe in a new Reformation as a real and exciting divine possibility.[5]

George Fox, the founder of Quakerism, who was among the new breed of his day, said that "there is one, even Jesus Christ, who can speak to thy condition." There still is, and He still can, if we are first able to speak with each other.

[5] *The New Reformation?* (Philadelphia: Westminster Press, 1965), p. 99.

chapter two

THE PROPHETIC VOICE

The most apparent characteristic of the new breed of Christian is a preoccupation with social action. Indeed, many young Christians will almost immediately discount (or to use the collegiate phrase, "turn off") any Christian spokesman who takes a "soft" line in the areas of civil rights, the war on poverty, and the peace movement. Paul Ramsey, for example, a distinguished and respected Christian ethicist, is regarded by some as a kind of traitor because of his general opposition to pulpiteering on specific social crimes. Thus, when a local minister says nothing about these issues, he is treated as if he had said something negative about them. The Christmas-basket approach to charity is regarded as mere tokenism at best and hypocrisy at worst. The church which says that it is, of course, against war but feels we must preserve freedom in Vietnam will not win much of a following among the dedicated (and sophisticated) young Christians of today. In no area is the new breed more critical, more outspoken, and more frustrated than in its feelings about the local church in *these* crucial areas.

In response to this reaction, some church members suggest serious steps of their own. Many advocate stopping financial support or firing the pastor or even starting new congregations. Many conscientious Christians, who at other times and as members of other generations have been socially concerned, respond with indignation and anger when confronted with the passionate and critical attitude of the new breed. Christians who fought the Ku Klux Klan when it was an influential political voice in many parts of the country —not just the South—scarcely react positively to civil rights advocates who demand more action by them now. Middle-aged Christians, who with Reinhold Niebuhr and others anguished through the naïveté of the social gospel and ran headlong into the harsh realities of nazism and communism, have several psychological barriers to overcome before they will be able to march on Washington to end the war in Vietnam—as the new breed seems to demand. Persons who survived the depression may not listen attentively to the affluent beatniks, who criticize the middle class for its lack of participation in the war on poverty. In short, the new breed—while not solely representing young persons— exhibits the impatience and generalizing tendencies of youth. The responsible Christian establishment (not including, in this instance, the several bigots, right-wingers, and militarists who seek religious support for their prejudices in our churches) does not always agree with the outspoken and seemingly radical attitudes of the new breed for what, to them, are valid reasons. Their experience and their perspective often make it difficult for them to sympathize with ideas that seem "way out." Thus, the gap between patient and impatient Christians, between young and told, between the cautious and the impetuous widens, and persons of good will end up frustrated with each other.

It is at this point that the Christian establishment will have to take its major step if it would narrow the gap between itself and its radical critics. While the local church has not been as socially unconcerned as its reputation leads us to believe, it still stands guilty of an indifference so acute that it has every reason to blush in embarrassment. A rejection of the church by this new breed of Christian is a prophetic judgment upon Christianity as it has been practiced by local churches in this country. The clichés of the racial revolution sting organized religion in this country because they ring true. "Eleven o'clock on Sunday morning *is* the most segregated hour of the week!" "The Church *has been* the taillight rather than the headlight of racial revolution." Such statements as these are mainly true, but even more relevant to this discussion is the fact that the new breed *believes* that they are true.

The war in Vietnam has caused many Christians to rethink their ideas about war in general. Is it a necessary evil or does it promote justice in some instances? Not since the pacifism of the early years of this century have so many Christians and would-be Christians agonized over what their position should be. However, while the rethinking has been going on, those Christians who demonstrate the "grace of impatience" are crying for the church to make a decision now about war and the sin of war. Perhaps Pierre Berton in his book *The Comfortable Pew* has been as typical and illustrative of this kind of criticism as any other.

Since the time of St. Augustine, the Christian Church, in which pacificism was initially a dominant idea, has lived with the concept of "the just and mournful war"—a war that the Church supports if the cause of one side is manifestly just and if the war is fought without vindictiveness. It was this concept that allowed the clergy in the two great world wars (not to mention the more abortive Crimean and Boer Wars) to utter a call to the colours. The unrestricted bombings and unconditional surrender terms of World War II seem to be to have made mincemeat of the "just war" argument, but it continues to be used in the nuclear age and is fairly obviously the basis of recent statement about deterrents and defence made by the Anglican Primate and the United Church Moderator. The argument for nuclear war is the same argument that was used in previous "just wars"—to wit, it can be condoned by Christians if its cause is moral, if the gains to be made are greater than the losses which appear likely, and if the warfare is conducted with "restraint" so that efforts are made not to endanger non-combatants. This is pretty well the position of the World Council of Churches, whose pronouncement in 1964 on the subject of disarmament was, in a memorable comment by Associated Press, "mild and calculated not to offend"—a phrase that might be taken as a slogan for the religious establishment in the age of the Bomb.[1]

[1] Pp. 23-24. From *The Comfortable Pew*, by Pierre Berton. Copyright © 1965 by Pierre Berton. Published by J. B. Lippincott Company and McClelland & Stewart, Limited, Toronto, and used by permission of the publishers.

The church has seemed to embrace man's inhumanity to man, and the rejection of it by the new breed may very well be evidence of God's judgment upon the churches. The judgment can be most keenly seen by the fact that that which, in general, the church has been calling upon its people to do for centuries is shaking the foundations. Churches in their official statements have always included a few paragraphs of support for the conscience of an occasional Christian who may object to war. When many of its most outspoken and best-educated members—indeed its leaders—take such a position, however, it doesn't quite know how to react.

What we must understand is that the new-breed Christians are profoundly *idealistic.* What so many conservative Christians have labeled "radicalism" is really a manifestation of idealism about the world and the obligations of the church. If older members and laymen have learned to live with the fact that the church is "a treasure in earthen vessels," the new breed is more attracted by the treasure than its container. The church has been telling its people that what the Lord requires is to "do justice, and to love kindness, and to walk humbly with God"; and now many within the Christian establishment are wondering what to do with this breed of people who are trying, at least, to do just these things!

The civil rights struggle captured the imagination and the loyalty of young Christians because it was a kind of "holy" struggle. It was the good guys vs. the bad guys, David against Goliath, poor Negroes pitted against Bull Connor.

It took a national crisis to make men reach. For years, the Negro protest has been driving organized religion toward one of those rare points of decision: Put up or shut up. Most Protestants had to recognize in the Negro, once black preachers forced the issue, a clear test of love and justice. But in order to respond, or refuse to, churchmen needed more than a vague gospel of social goodness and moralistic prohibitions against sex and drink. Only self-immersion into the complex person of Christ, as theologians had been saying, could provide the cues. You had to ask yourself, as one Birmingham Sunday school teacher did, "Where would Christ be?" [2]

The war on poverty, too, represents a kind of final frontier in America for idealists to demonstrate compassion and understanding. While the rugged individualist within the church frets over wasting tax money and perpetuating laziness, the new breed focuses upon the humanitarian concern over what is involved in being poor. Hunger is a tangible problem, and seeing to it that hungry babies are fed is more important than balancing the budget or being efficient. This is the way the new breed thinks. This is why some—though not by any means all—college students dress shabbily, or become beatniks or "grubs." They are seeking, by the way they dress, to identify with the poor. They want to be a walking commentary on, and criticism of, the middle-class values which frequently and knowingly reject persons who are victims of poverty. While such actions by concerned students in a college which costs three thousand dollars a year to attend may seem ludicrous, they do reflect how very concerned many students are about this issue.

An important distinction needs to be made, of course, between two kinds of radicals who stand out by virtue of their dress or their opposition to the norms of society. One kind, represented in the extreme by the so-called hippie, has rejected society. He has dropped out. He doesn't care what people think of him, and he—through drugs, or by living a kind of underground existence—avoids the sins and dilemmas of our society. The other kind is the activist. He wants to change the world. He believes very deeply in democracy, to the extent that he fights against what he regards as fascist tendencies in America. He often regards America as the greatest humanitarian nation in the world, and he seeks to help keep it that way. He lobbies, demonstrates, marches, sits in, and speaks out. His goal is to help his country live up to its own best ideals. New-breed Christians are always sympathetic to the second kind of radical, and in their own way they seek to help their churches live up to the standards of the gospel. A certain activist collegian was perfectly willing to shed his beard and cut his hair in order to "get clean for Gene" in the Senator's presidential campaign. Once he became convinced, rightly or wrongly, that there was a man worth working for, the idealism of his position became dominant and apparent.

Perhaps in no area is the idealism of the new breed more apparent than in their passionate concern for peace. A significant percentage of the participants in the marches on Washington, New York, San Francisco, and other cities are almost always young clergymen or seminarians. Also included are a number of young mothers and college students, who, when questioned, say they are there out of Methodist, Episcopal, Quaker, or other Christian concern. By no means are all participants in peace efforts present out of religious motivation, as many who are disenchanted with the Church would carefully disavow any connection with it. However, to the chagrin of those persons who would prefer to think that peace movements are synonymous with subversion, the fact is that they are much more illustrative of idealism than communism.

The extent of the new breed's concern for peace is indicated, furthermore, by the consistency of their point of view as expressed by other spokesmen. Anti-Vietnam-War sentiments are stated regularly by *The Christian Century, Renewal Magazine, Christianity and Crisis,* and *Between the Lines.* These are the journals which "radical" Christians trust, and they differ only as to which radical steps must be taken to resolve the conflict. Significantly, these journals have a loyal following because the concerned Christian is convinced that they can be trusted; but the new breed feels the mass media, for the most part, are controlled or dominated by "party lines" or hypocritical attitudes.

Young Christians, let it be remembered, regard Vietnam as an avoidable war, at least, and certainly not one that conjures up flag-flying feelings of patriotism. Old-breed Christians mark a closer identification between the will of God and the will of the nation. Walter Lippmann, however, has probably put the feelings of younger Christians into words in his well-publicized comment, "Old men shouldn't start wars that young men have to fight." It should not be construed, however, that young Christians are simply pleading for a greater voice in such decisions. Fundamental to their objection is the belief that the war in Vietnam rages now because of national pride, the greed of the military-industrial complex, and crude political motivation.

The idealism of these Christians, not a lack of patriotism, is the fact that other Christians must take seriously, if they are to be understood. That idealism is a judgment upon us all. Activism is the soul brother of idealism, of course, and the new breed is a generation of doers. The church is regarded as being content with platitudes, but the Christian representatives of the "now" generation admire action much more than words. In so many words, activist Christians want answers from the church establishment to two crucial questions: (1) What are *you doing* in God's name for your neighbor? (2) What do you have for *me to do* for him?

Thus, as local churches timidly plan such baby steps as having pulpit exchanges on Race Relations Sunday, the new breed is attracted to government programs such as Operation Head Start, the Job Corps, and Upward Bound. On the college campuses, for example, there is some interest in worship, some in discussion, and a little in retreats. However, literally hundreds of students sign up for work camps, tutoring projects with disadvantaged children, and other activist concerns. This stress on activism is the reason why new-breed idealism is such a clear judgment upon the churches. Local churches are active as they can be, but their activities are often part of the problem, not part of the answer. They are saying the right things ("we're for peace but—"), and their lack of tangible follow-through in projects and activities in the areas of peace, civil rights, and poverty indicates hypocrisy—and causes the churches to be less acceptable to the new breed than if they had said nothing at all.

One group of activitist Christians, for example, literally laughed aloud at the newsletter which came from the home church of one of its members. The striking thing about the article in question was the great inappropriateness of the language used to describe a project which seemed to them silly and self-centered.

The whole New Testament says our concern must be expressed in love. This is the story of how one group of young women in Urbanville Community (name changed to protect the guilty) expressed their concern for their church in *love,* and had the *courage and faith to follow through.*

One October Sunday in 1957, a member of the Gregarian Group of the Christian Women's Fellowship, had an urge for her group to do *something really worthwhile* for their church. She talked with her pastor about it. They decided that starting a fund for *new pew cushions,* to replace the old faded, torn, and soiled ones, would be a worthy project. When Marie proposed it at the next group meeting, it was voted unanimously. It cost several thousand dollars but the Gregarians had the courage to go ahead, and they began planning their project.

The irony of churches using words like "courage" and "faith" to describe efforts to make sitting down easier was not lost on the group!

Indeed, the irrelevance of the local church is at the heart of the problem—in the minds of the new breed. The kind of church which captures the imagination of these Christians is the Church of the Saviour in Washington, D.C., or Judson Memorial Church in New York City. Part of the reason that these churches have such dynamic programs of activities is, of course, that New York and Washington have more problems, more resources, and more opportunities than Podunk Pond, New York, or Spiceland, Indiana. At this point many critical Christians are unrealistic, and their idealism gets in the way of practical opportunities. Still, there is scarcely any argument by the enormous churches which have huge budgets and little outreach of social concern that can justify their existence in the mind of a great many Christians. As one church dropout put it, "Why should I support a church which has as its main project each year a fair to raise money to support the church which has as its main project a fair to raise money?" The rebuttal question, which members of the church establishment properly may ask, is: "Why don't you get in there and change things?" This question will be met by a shrug, and perhaps the shrug is a more realistic response than the question; for many among the new breed know how inflexible and rigid the patterns of local churches are, or can be.

The fact is that many of the new breed do a better job of implementing their ideals than the local church does. Headlines tell of beer-drinking students running wild in Florida resorts during the Easter holidays, but a significant minority have been spending their spring vacations in work-camp projects in deprived areas. For example, nearly two hundred college men and women from a half-dozen California universities and colleges worked in Mexico during spring vacation, building schools and centers for handicapped children. The idea for the Easter work-pilgrimage was inspired by a petite twenty-five-year-old Seattle girl, who had been working on a church project in Mexicali. When she discovered that there was no schooling available for deaf and blind children in nearby Tijuana, she got in touch with several campus leaders in California. Notice that she did not contact the pastor of her local church (or maybe she did—without results!). She went to the source where she thought she could get the most help.

The new breed literally threw their bodies into Mississippi Freedom Summer during the height of civil rights activity in the South, and more recently into a massive project called Vietnam Summer, in which a broad-based attack on the war in Vietnam was carried on. Christian students joined with many others whose motivations were simply political or humanitarian; but to the Christian the *doing* of the "right" thing was, and is, more important than worrying about the credentials of their colleagues in these efforts. Idealism and activism have brought these Christians into working relationships with people concerned for the "right" causes, and for the new breed this is what matters.

There is one other aspect of practical idealism which marks this breed of Christian and distinguishes him from past youthful reformers and idealists. Vital Christians of today are little interested in "band-aid" Christianity. They want to be involved in major surgery, in efforts and programs that will make a difference over the long haul. In this sense, they are not wide-eyed idealists; rather, these Christians demonstrate a kind of *sophistication* not typical of their counterparts in the past. They are keenly aware of political realities, of the power structure of the community, and of the specialized efforts of the government in social action. These avenues, they feel, are more sensible and in the long run more effective than well-intentioned charity and sincere afterthoughts. Roger L. Shinn, in his insightful little book *Tangled World,* describes the situation of which the new breed is much more aware than the church establishment seems to be.

Our world is full of examples. Some of the striking ones come from international affairs. Sometimes the American people, moved by a combination of self-interest and good will, have tried to help another country suffering from poverty. Churches and other voluntary agencies have sent people and money. Congress, with its usual reluctance, has voted economic aid. The Peace Corps has given educational and engineering help. Everybody regarded these as ethical acts. But while all this was going on, a change of one cent a pound in the prices of coffee and cocoa did more harm to the economy than all the efforts to help it. Nobody regarded the price change as an ethical issue; in fact it represented no decision at all. It resulted from many unpredictable events—the size of crops, changes in shipping costs, maybe a labor controversy or two, a shift of housewives' preferences from regular to instant coffee. These miscellaneous forces, which have no ethical purpose, so changed vast organizational processes as to wipe out a deliberate moral effort of people and governments.[8]

Shinn goes on to say this: "In every discussion of social problems somebody sooner or later says: 'The way to get a better world is to get better people,' or 'the answer to that social problem [war, racial tensions, disputes between capital and labor] is to change the

[8] (New York: Charles Scribner's Sons, 1965), p. 58.

hearts of men.' By this time in history that judgment has surely been proved wrong. . . . We need better institutions to implement human generosity, to thwart human evil, and to channel organizational processes that unintentionally hurt as well as help people." Christians of genuine intellectual sophistication are more willing than ever before to serve God in other than traditional ways. A person with sophisticated and keen understanding of what it means to be a Christian businessman, a Christian economist, a Christian politician, or a Christian scientist can actually *do more* for the kingdom of God in given instances than many ministers, missionaries, or social workers. While, in fact, there may be relatively few Christians in a position to affect the price of coffee (and indirectly meet the human needs of thousands), the awareness of these kinds of interrelationships clearly affects the understanding by the new breed of what it "means" to be a Christian in twentieth-century society.

A more sophisticated understanding of the dynamics of race and poverty, of minority groups and needs, has stimulated many Christians to throw themselves into certain causes with passionate enthusiasm. Seminarians enter the world now with a background in psychology that was never dreamed of twenty-five years ago. Many schools have been exposing their students to the realities of the ghetto with greater success than they have the realities of the white, Protestant, suburban ghettos. Thus, young clergymen seek to integrate communities because they can see the consequences of not integrating them. They see the importance of following leaders like the late Martin Luther King because the alternatives are so much worse. They seek to provide job opportunities for the poor because the connection between unemployment and riots is unmistakable. Charles A. Wells, who has proved himself to be a reliable prophet for several years, demonstrates this kind of insight in his newsletter *Between the Lines.* In commenting about the dilemma of Negro soldiers in Vietnam, he writes:

With only one-year service in Vietnam required, it won't be long before a million men will have been in Vietnam—which means approximately 250,000 Negro veterans, most of them conscious they have served in the most painful and deadly areas of the conflict which most "whiteys" were able to avoid. (Including U.S. Naval forces, there are nearly 500,000 Americans in Vietnam now and have been for many months.) Are we to assume that a quarter of a million Negro service men, trained and hardened in the arts of violence, and painfully conscious of how they have been exploited at home during peace and abroad during the war, can be restored to our racially torn communities without a change of tempo? They will present a different attitude from that of the somewhat gentle "Deacons of Defense," Negro householders who, arming themselves, have put quite a crimp in the KKK throughout the South. There is also much to be said about the Black Muslim movement in this connection, for the returning Negro veterans will find it much more compatible with their feeling than the defensiveness of the soft-spoken Deacons.[4]

The knowledge explosion of our time, when tempered and guided by the New Testament, becomes an "insight explosion." The significant prophets of the twentieth century have exchanged their hair shirts and

[4] *Between the Lines,* May 1, 1967.

loincloths for striped ties, Harris tweed jackets, and a briefcase full of sociological texts. The prophets for this century are men and women of our time, and sophisticated Christians recognize them as such.

What ought the response of local churches be to these prophetic voices? Certainly, as we have already said, it will have to be something other than it has been—a reaction of suspicion ("they're communist!") or indifference ("we have to meet our own church budget first"). Many individual Christians are feeling the impact of the new breed on their family units, as they wake up to discover that they have reared children who have become better Christians than they expected —or, perhaps, even wanted. They are positively shocked when their sons seek 1-0 classification in the draft and are willing to face the disgrace of becoming conscientious objectors. Parents frequently do not know how to react to their sons' eagerness to work for little pay in the inner city. Why can't they become nice, decent engineers or professional people, who live by the side of the road and are friends to man?

To ignore the prophetic insights of the new breed, however, is to discount the value of the salt to the flavor of the steak. In the realm of social witness these Christians are the leaven. They are part of the answer to a much greater degree than they are part of the problem. They have—at this point in history—more to tell the establishment than it has to tell them. They are the conscience of the church, and the church dares not stifle their still, small voices.

Local churches and some denominations are taking these prophetic insights seriously. Some churches have started programs of providing low-cost loans, handled through the church treasurer, to aid Negroes and low-economic-level families in moving out of their ghettos. Individual Christians have served as anonymous middlemen to assist middle-class Negro families in moving into middle-class residential areas. Some congregations have become involved in setting up halfway houses for the re-entry of prisoners into society. A very few churches have been able to make any important statements about the war in Vietnam. However, many Christians, who are active members of congregations which the new breed call irrelevant or "stuffy," have made such statements and matched them with corresponding actions.

People with such reactions as these take seriously the prophetic witness of the more radical "leaven," and can serve as evidence that the local church has not lost all its sense of social concern. The probability is that the local church will never really capture the fancy of radical Christians, because it is not equipped or psychologically oriented toward activist projects such as demonstrations, marches, vigils, sit-ins, and the like. Its best opportunity is to respond in ways that are congenial to its own collective psyche—the "practical" ways that can be sold to a conservative mind and yet are clearly part of the "right" causes. Credit unions, such as were mentioned above, and organizations to integrate housing are illustrations of responsible reactions. The church must be true to itself, and its guilt lies, not in its refusal to picket, but in its unwillingness to use its own peculiar resources and good sense in facing the crucial social concerns of our time. Thus, the church (we mean primarily its leaders) must seek to *challenge the minds and hearts* of most of its members.

47

Too often the clergy has simply reflected the attitudes of the church's members, and often, its most conservative ones. Church rolls are full of people with vested interests, and the task of confronting their attitudes is a prime one for church leaders. Certainly, the church does not have the luxury of thinking that its members are already dedicated Christians in the realm of social action. They are not. They are often closed channels, and their religion may well be used as an endorsement for their narrowness.

The church, however, needs to evaluate its own concern (or lack of it) as well as its responses to its radical members according to certain criteria: (1) Is the concern for *persons* clearly indicated? As the *Peanuts* cartoon makes clear, it is possible to "love" mankind while hating people. Thus the church cannot legitimately refuse involvement in social causes because an inefficient use of money is at stake—unless a more efficient means of demonstrating a concern for people is available. Many radical Christians, too, have found themselves shoulder to shoulder in great causes with people who are personally difficult to live with. Concern for persons is the criterion for social action that the church can insist upon. (2) The church is not married simply to causes. It will be involved in causes (hopefully the right ones) so long as it exists, but it must continue to be seeking the will of God in given situations. Those persons, both within the church and without, who make their religion simply a *cause,* miss a crucial point. There are some Quakers, for example, whose religion is the quest for peace, and if war could somehow be eliminated, their religion would cease to be. Likewise, some good Methodists and Baptists have

48

identified Christianity with temperance, and if booze ever ceased to be a problem, their religion would be bankrupt. The standard by which radical and conservative Christians alike must judge themselves is the *eternal dimension* of social action. We are not married to causes, but we are dedicated to respond to God's leading in history now. Failure of a cause ought not to lead to an employment problem among Christians; there is always a new call to a new service for the living God.

As the church seeks to respond to the new breed, it must evaluate its action—or inaction—by these criteria. On a more practical level, churches can evaluate themselves in terms of their balance between message and mission. Both are necessary, and a stress on one at the expense of another can emasculate any would-be Christian witness. The time has passed when local churches can think of themselves as the most active social agent in the community. The time has also passed wherein they can stand about and worry whether or not they are being distinctive or preserving their unique witness. The time has come, hastened by the new breed, wherein the local church will have to search its collective conscience. The bulk of society is perfectly willing to let the church be the custodian of the *status quo*. However, those elements which cry out for help will also be heard. Many church members have been able to rationalize their lack of concern for people by using theology, common sense, and an appeal to a balanced budget—but the new breed will have none of this. The local church must now recognize that it faces the judgment of God—the Christian God—who calls us to comfort the afflicted and afflict the comfortable. Anything less than this will alienate the next generation of Christians—the children of the new breed—beyond reprieve. This condition we cannot afford, for no church can exist without its conscience.

QUESTIONS FOR DISCUSSION

1. Here is a letter to the editor of a metropolitan newspaper:

"What's wrong with the churches?" or "What's wrong with the clergy?" is the theme of countless letters to the editor and of editorials in newspapers and other publications all over the United States.

I think the question should be instead, "What's wrong with members of the churches that permit the erratic behavior of the clericals to continue?"

A good starting point would be the fundamental question, who is working for whom? While millions of church members complain, they go to church or in many cases no longer attend, but dutifully continue to contribute their financial support. If they still believe in either heaven or hell, they should be reminded that a check book is not a ticket for either gate.

Increasing numbers of congregations whose denominations are affiliated with the National Council of Churches, are reducing or withholding entirely financial support of their judicatories.

To do these things takes courage but since when has it not taken courage to stand up for Christian convictions.

The Fletchers, the Malcolm Boyds, the Blakes, the Pikes and other misguided clericals, many of whom have preached violation of the law, can flourish only in an atmosphere of congregational apathy and indifference."

Is this an appropriate response? Would the church be better or worse off if the radicals and their followers were squelched? What is the point beyond which a person should no longer support his local church? When it supports financially the National Council of Churches? When it refuses membership to a Negro? Never, under any circumstances?

2. What is your reaction to the quotation from Pierre Berton's *The Comfortable Pew* on p. 34? Is there such a thing in a nuclear age as a "just war"? In your opinion, has the United States ever fought a war in its history which was not "just"? What ought to be the position of local churches toward their youth who seek to be conscientious objectors? Ostracism (because they embarrass the congregation)? Moral support (as an expression of appreciation for the right of individual conscience)? What ought to be the attitude of the church toward involvement in military service? Should pacifism be taught as a "live" alternative? Discuss the criteria for being a Christian soldier; how is he different from a "non-Christian" soldier?

3. Do you agree with the *Look* magazine article that the Negro protest was a "clear test of love and justice"? (See p. 36.) Do you think that in time white Christians would have come around to integrating buses, schools, public facilities, and neighborhoods? Have the riots been a result of the success of demonstrations, i.e., an inevitable consequence of assuming that legal procedures will not produce results? When, if ever, should Christians violate laws? Were Christians who shared in the underground railway that helped to free slaves acting properly? Should German Christians have supported Hitler in his treatment of the Jews? Would sit-ins, demonstrations, etc., have been necessary if Christians in local churches had embraced the cause of civil rights earlier?

4. "An ever-growing number of young American men are finding that the American war in Vietnam so outrages their deepest moral and religious sense that they cannot contribute to it in any way. We share their moral outrage. . . . Especially we call upon the universities to fulfill their mission of enlightenment and religious organizations to honor their heritage of brotherhood. Now is the time to resist."

Is the war in Vietnam a "special" war? Why do some Christians speak of their "moral outrage"? How can a local church be critical of the war in Vietnam and still minister to the families of servicemen?

5. See the quotation from Roger Shinn, p. 43. Do you agree with this? What persons in your congregation are in positions which can affect the welfare of many others by virtue of their business decisions?

6. What firsthand contacts do members of your group (church) have with the poor and disadvantaged of your community? What factors brought about this contact or lack of it?

7. How would you evaluate your local church by the criteria on p. 48? (a) Does it have a concern for persons —all persons, regardless of race, color, or economic status? How is this concern manifest? (b) Is your church married to a cause? What are the social causes that the established churches over the years have found acceptable? Temperance? Anti-gambling? Sexual immorality? Are these different in kind from civil rights, peace, and poverty? Is there a difference between personal morality and social morality?

8. Examine the budget and reports of your congregation over the last five years. Is the main concern *internal* (buildings, maintenance, ministry, denomination), or *external* (persons in need, foreign missions, social action)?

BIBLIOGRAPHY

Berton, Pierre. *The Comfortable Pew*. Philadelphia: J. B. Lippincott, 1965.

Cox, Harvey. *The Secular City*. New York: The Macmillan Co., 1965.

Mullen, Thomas J. *The Ghetto of Indifference*. Nashville: Abingdon Press, 1966.

Rose, Stephen C., *Who's Killing the Church?* New York: Association Press, 1966.

Stringfellow, William. *My People Is the Enemy*. New York: Holt, Rinehart & Winston, 1964.

chapter three

THE SEARCH FOR SEXUAL INTEGRITY

Of the writing of books and articles about sex, there seems to be no end. Much of what is written shocks older Christians in established churches, not just because it is too liberal, but because it is being written in the name of the church or by persons who carry Christian credentials. Joseph Fletcher, author of *Situation Ethics,* is a teacher in an accredited seminary, for Pete's sake, and Richard Hettlinger, who says some very permissive things in his *Living With Sex,* is a college chaplain! As we have seen, such news is too great a burden for many Christians to bear, and many are ready to call for an investigation by the Unchristian Activities Committee of the church.

Before this happens, however, we urge restraint. This is a problem which looks worse from a distance than it does up close, and it is important that concerned Christians see the difference between what responsible spokesmen about sexual morality among the new breed are saying and what other contemporary spokesmen, who do *not* speak from a Christian perspective, are saying. There is, after all, an observable difference between what Joseph Fletcher says about sex and what Hugh Hefner writes in *Playboy* magazine. It is often a difference in emphasis, but primarily it is a difference in perspective. No avowed Christian seriously advocates sexual freedom without the complement of responsibility—and this almost always means marriage. For Hefner, it simply doesn't mean marriage "almost always."

Indeed, spokesmen for the new morality delight in debating with persons like Hefner and Albert Ellis, as they see sharp differences in their general points of view. There is, in other words, a difference between being "liberal" about sex and being "libertine" about it. However, because the debate, in fact, takes place and because the differences among several of the more newsworthy statements about sex are not often made clear, the conscientious churchman who values virginity and decency very highly sometimes feels he has been sold out by a new breed of Christian.

This is not the case, and while many of us can disagree with aspects of the "new morality," it is important that we understand *why* its proponents are saying what they are saying about sexual relationships. They are seeing and hearing young people while they are involved in a painful search for sexual integrity. They are starting from where the young people are, and where they are is in the middle of groups who are questioning virginity, the condemnation of homosexuality, the institution of marriage, the nature of love, and the whole style of life of middle-class, white Anglo-Saxon Americans. No longer do these Christians regard the discussion of sexual morality as a simple one of "do you or don't you?" To understand what they are saying, we must also understand *why* they are saying the liberal things they are.

OUR TIME OF SEXUAL FREEDOM

Persons who are twenty now have been brought up in a radically different sexual context than were people even ten or fifteen years older. The last ten years have been a period of sexual bombardment in America. On every side we are deluged by sex in one form or another. This is especially true in the realm of "spectator sex"—those forms of it which may be seen and read. Not long ago the writing of John O'Hara was criticized as being "sex-obsessed," but now he appears positively platonic alongside a John Updike, who describes lyrically, and in detail, matters that used to be mentioned only in Latin. Our enlightened age has also been treated to such works as William Burroughs' *Naked Lunch,* an incredible piece of hallucinatory homosexual depravity, and other literary efforts of equal stature. By a strenuous stretching of the imagination, these works may be classified as literature (and perhaps they are), but outnumbering them on the bosom racks are such scintillating titles as *Lust Hop, Lust Jungle, Lust Kicks, Lust Lover, Lust Lease, Lust Moll, Lust Team,* and *Lust Girls,* to name a group of titles on one well-stocked literary counter. Indeed, should one be an identifiable Christian such as a clergy-man, he finds it almost necesary to don dark glasses, a black trench coat, and a false mustache to acquire enough nerve to buy a newspaper at the corner drug-store. Spectator sex is wilder than ever before.

The young adults of our time have been guided through their teen years in this kind of atmosphere. They have been exposed to Hefner's law which says that intercourse before and/or outside marriage is valuable "under the right conditions." Albert Ellis may have been invited to their college campuses to speak on his theme that society should consider elimi-nating marriage and substituting temporary "relation-ships" with no strings attached. Or the young adults may have read Margaret Mead's statements advocating that coeducational nudity at certain times and places is better that the American obsession with public near-nudity which now exists.

To expect the new breed of Christian to be insulated from such ideas or from people who accept the ideas at face value is unreasonable. An occasional artistic (as opposed to pornographic) book, poem, play, or movie that could not have been produced even ten years ago causes the new breed to hesitate before em-bracing censorship. The casual and uninhibited style of dress, which shocks the elders, is taken rather for granted by many among the new breed of Christian, or pagan. Indeed, Earl H. Brill, writing in *The Chris-tian Century,* indicates through satire this sexual gener-ation gap:

Look for example at the way college girls dress. Their short short skirt made the springtime campus blossom into a veritable skin show (at least by the standards of my own youth). You might suppose that this indicates an increasing sex-consciousness, but you would be quite mistaken: it means the very opposite.

For in fact the creeping nudity of female fashions goes quite unnoticed by the young men. To most of them it doesn't occur to give a second look at a well turned thigh. Not so with their elders. I have been conducting a little poll among my colleagues and it means that they (let's be honest—*we*) are the overage beneficiaries of the new landscape. We were brought up in the sexual age and we will keep the faith. But the young men fail to appreciate the aesthetic delights of their environment.[1]

In this way, and in other more important ones, the generation from which the new breed of Christian draws most of its members starts from a different set of assumptions about sex.

Therefore, internal dissension breaks loose as Christians wrestle with their own dilemmas about sexual morality in the mid-twentieth century. Those who expect the church to be the bastion of fidelity and sexual abstinence before marriage are disturbed that some Christians see the issue as a fuzzy one. They may be surprised and taken back at such actions as that of the British Council of Churches which recently appointed a committee whose task it was to make a report on sex and morality. The committee refused to condemn outright either premarital intercourse or adultery. Thus, if Christians are to communicate with each other—much less with the world—about sexual

[1] "Sex Is Dead!" Copyright 1966 Christian Century Foundation. Reprinted by permission from the August 3, 1966 issue of *The Christian Century*.

morality, we first have to recognize that our day is a new day. Whether it is a better day is clearly open to debate, but there is no question that it is a different one.

EXPOSURE TO LIFE

A second reason why sexual questions seem more complex to the new breed of Christian is his increased exposure to life—life in the raw, in the slum, among the disadvantaged, or among the problem persons of our society.

Radical churchmen are influenced by the nature of the new ministries in which many of them are involved. Because of their intense social concern, they have come to have more contact with victims of poverty, racial discrimination, and a disadvantaged environment. Because of their stress upon the church in the world, they have had more contact than ever before with certain "special" categories of people—the alcoholic, the dope addict, the artist, the alienated. William Stringfellow describes in his book *My People Is the Enemy* how he felt that his identification with the people of his Harlem slum was complete when a Negro hustler offered his girl friend to him for sexual purposes. Stringfellow, in other words, felt that this particularly casual and "immoral" attitude toward sex was less important than other problems "his" people faced. To be an effective attorney in their behalf, he felt he could not judge their sexual habits at that point.

Similar so-called libertine attitudes are demonstrated by Christians in the world who are seeking to work with and help homosexuals. They become concerned about such persons to a degree that makes it virtually impossible for them to regard homosexuality as mere perversion or simple sin. They come to regard it as sickness, and thus they are more tolerant of it in their public statements. Christian social workers may even come to have a kind of tolerant respect for the ADA Negro mother who allows a man to live with her and her family without benefit of clergy—when this arrangement helps pay the bills and meet the pressing fundamental needs of the family. Social workers come to appreciate the fact that some illiterate and unskilled women will do even "this" for the sake of preserving their families. Many counselors and chaplains, both within and without the university, may take what seems to be a too-liberal attitude toward abortion, but the reason they do so may be that they have identified closely with young girls who find themselves in trouble because they were stupid or naïve. Birth control pills, dispensed to unmarried women through a clinic in the slums, may be a better solution than illegitimate babies so far as the problem of sex in that environment is concerned.

In short, as Christians identify more closely and passionately with the problems of the world, their attitudes toward people who have become victims of the power of sex almost inevitably become more tolerant. They may find themselves loving the sinner considerably more than they hate the sin. They may even react against middle-class smugness and piety about sex to the extent that their own people (white Anglo-Saxon Protestants) become their "enemies."

This does not mean, of course, that free love should necessarily be endorsed by the church, nor does it mean that birth control pills should be distributed to the college girl swinger, who naïvely thinks of sex as mere fun and games. It merely means that part of the reason why Christians differ so much on sexual morality these days is because their daily working experiences vary tremendously.

No wonder many Christians, when asked what is right or wrong, respond with the question: "That depends. What is the situation?"

THE PERSONAL NATURE OF SEX

Experiencing life in intensely personal ways is part of the cry of the new generation of young adults around the world, and Christians are part of this thrust, too. The hippie has to do "his thing." The literature assigned in college classes is often existentialist and personal. That which is true but *irrelevant* to the individual is often discounted. In the realm of morality some Christians have discovered that sexual relationships are experienced in different ways by different people.

Because sex is a tremendously personal matter, it is nearly impossible to spell out in strict and inflexible ways how one should deal with it and express it. One's moral upbringing, his toilet training, his overall emotional stability, his environment, the relationship he has had with his parents—these and many other factors will affect how a person feels about sexual expressions of many different kinds and degrees. Some people come from kissing families; all the relatives participate in an orgy of hello and farewell kissing every Thanksgiving, Christmas, and family wedding. Other families may

61

have no outward or public expression of affection. Many of us have known persons who have said that they could never remember seeing their parents embrace in front of them. This situation makes it difficult indeed for one person to tell another person precisely how the other individual should treat sexual expressions. Sexual intercourse, within marriage as well as outside it, means different things to different people. For some, it is a "fate worse than death." For others, "it is one of those things."

Radical Christians, in fact, criticize a libertine attitude about sex on the very grounds that persons with such a viewpoint are not taking seriously the intensely personal nature of a sexual relationship. They disagree with a person such as Albert Ellis, who advocates a kind of code which is often an extension of one's own feelings and not a realistic appraisal of personal differences. Dr. Ellis, in over a dozen books and two hundred articles, encourages—even urges—young Americans to perpetrate almost any sexual act their cunning minds can devise. Above all, Ellis preaches against feeling guilty or remorseful. "Peace of mind lies in promiscuity, salvation in sin, sanity in seduction," says one commentator as he evaluates this attitude. Ellis offers what amounts to a sexual code: do anything sexual you wish, as long as you do not do it with a minor, do not use mental or physical coercion, do not conceive an unwanted child, and, above all, do not feel guilty. The tragic error in this attitude is, oddly enough, the same error that the sexually inhibited, overly strict parent makes: *One simply does not know what the other person's reaction will be, and, in fact, one cannot always predict what one's own reaction to a given sexual experience will be.*

More often than not, the new-breed Christian counselors end up cautioning young adults against premarital and extramarital sex. They hold out for the exception, however, and for the occasional situation which does not fit an inflexible pattern. They continue to stress the value of persons in sexual relationship, and on this point they are (although unwilling to admit it) very orthodox.

THE GLORIFICATION OF "HONESTY"

With a stress on the personal nature of sexual relationships, it follows that the new breed would see "honesty" as a keystone of sexual ethics. The "permissive" writers on situation ethics are certainly not saying that "everything goes if you're in love." They usually are not talking about erotic love at all. They are speaking of the kind and quality of love that seeks nothing for itself but simply obeys the Christian commandment to "love one's neighbor as oneself." In a matter as variable and intensely personal as sexual relationships, such love means that we seek at all times the highest welfare of the other person as well as our own. Richard Hettlinger, chaplain at Kenyon College, is seemingly sometimes permissive toward intercourse outside marriage in special circumstances. Yet in his book *Living With Sex* he says that "there is danger of complete chaos and untold disaster unless those who claim to order their actions by love instead of law are absolutely honest in examining their motives critically." Honesty is vital, completely necessary, and no substitutes for it are acceptable.

The problem, of course, is that people are notably unable to be objective about their own sex lives. No sphere of life is more sensitive, more vulnerable, or more directly a part of the center of ourselves. Joseph Fletcher, in a magazine interview, was asked if the new morality will lead to license. His answer is significant: "I do fear it. Sex is dynamite. In the past we have tried to guard against this dynamite through legalistic controls. Now we are going to have to look for positive rather than negative commandments; for devotion to an ideal rather than to fear of consequences." Many among the new breed are honestly recognizing the power of sex, but they are also afraid of the legalistic and negative stand toward it which has typified the church in the past. Practically no Christian spokesmen on the topic come out in favor of license or irresponsibility. Honesty about sex and its power, and honesty about the dangers of a negative understanding of sex, need to be shared by Christians of many persuasions.

A CRITICISM OF "RESPECTABLE" SOCIETY

The new breed of Christian still regards marriage as the normative state for sexual relationships. Sex and marriage still go together. There is general agreement on this point, not simply because this is the way it has always been, but because love can best be served when loyalty and commitment to the other person are built into the relationship. At the same time, marriage in the United States of America, with all its respectable and proper overtones, is so badly tarnished that it is open to serious criticism. "Proper" sexual morality, too, seems to many among the new breed to be sham and hypocrisy.

Marriage, some say, is often legalized cohabitation, and many married persons have nothing important to say to each other. By contrast, some young adults may find, before marriage, a better relationship than that of their churchgoing parents. The idealism of the new breed comes through, too, as they look with disapproval —or even disgust—at the crass materialism, status consciousness, and self-seeking which permeate middle-class America. What right, they say, does this group have to criticize any young person's sexual mores?

This attitude was clearly demonstrated in a conversation with two recent college graduates, who had just seen the controversial movie *The Graduate*. They felt strongly that the young couple in the movie were justified in their efforts to get together, bizarre as they were, because their relationship was pure and good, while that of their parents was false, hypocritical, and spiritually bankrupt. The family situations, as portrayed in the movie, were, indeed, like this, and the question then became whether or not the relationships described were typical of upper-middle-class respectable America. More often than not, this young couple felt, *they* are typical! Furthermore, the young people were declared Christians, and they were seriously considering going on to seminary.

The point is that there is much about American marriage, which *seems* to have the blessing of the church, that the new breed can rightly criticize. A search for sexual integrity from now on will have to involve a better alternative than marrying for the wrong reasons or merely fulfilling society's expectations. That kind of marriage is simply not good enough for the new breed of Christians, and getting married just to legalize a sexual relationship is not good enough, either. In the dialogue about sex we must include conversations about the nature of marriage in depth. The church cannot seem to give its blessings to marriages which simply meet legal and social requirements and still expect to win the respect of Christians involved in the search for genuine sexual integrity.

Sexual experiences *can* be a part of a total life-experience, and Christians can unite around the effort to put sex into the proper context. Sexual intercourse can be a way of saying "I love you at every level of my being!" and promoting this idea with integrity and purposefulness should be high on the list of every Christian regardless of his credentials.

It may be that if we listen to each other, we will be better equipped to answer the hardest question that any conscientious Christian has to face: when are we to be strict and firm, and when are we to be forgiving and flexible? Certainly the dialogue on sexual morality will produce a greater sense of compassion for the sexual sinner and more yoking together of that compassion with realistic action. Many churches in England have supported the Wolfenden Report, which urged that "homosexual behavior between consenting adults in private should not longer be a criminal offense." There may be started more realistic efforts to help unwed mothers. The churches may come to support connubial visits for prisoners, or those churches which have strict divorce laws may relax them somewhat.

We may find ourselves giving greater attention to

the forgotten majority, too, and we may find ways of making clear that the vast mass of people who face sexual temptations before, after, or during marriage will end up practicing monogamy, fidelity, and pre-marital abstinence—if they wish really to affirm the existence and value of the other persons they claim to love. Can Christians agree about the rule, and then concentrate the debate on the exceptions?

The fact that Christians are confused about sexual morality ought not to surprise us, but neither should it discourage us and drive us back into the cocoon of our own rigidly established, preconceived positions, be they liberal or conservative. We may be able to lift our heads above the fog of confusion from time to time to realize that there are many reasons for thanksgiving *because* of our dilemma. We may be able to say "thank God" for the pill which makes it possible for persons to be more responsible parents than ever before. Some of us clearly want to thank God for the new freedom, which allows a woman to view sex as something more noble than a duty and a man to regard it as more than his right. Thank God, if we can be more understanding of people whose ability to be sexual beings is hampered, and if we can go beyond branding them with scarlet letters of condemnation. We can be grateful for more honesty about sex, more naturalness about our bodies, and more freedom to be honest. Thank God for the fruits of the new morality.

Our thanksgiving, however, does not stop there. We may contemplate our own lives and say a word of thanksgiving for rules and regulations which may have kept opportunity for sexual experimentation from us when we were too young to handle its power. Most of us rejoice as we think of the marriage vows we took and the commitment we made which has put sex in the best possible context for fulfillment. We thank God for the external mores of society which help sustain us when we fall "out of love." We thank him for the truth that loyalty, and not just passion, is demanded by Christian marriage, so that we do not walk away from each other when bored or when a given sexual experience fails to give us either joy or excitement. Thanks be to God for the "squares," whose inhibitions have encouraged us to be inhibited when we may have needed to be.

God has given us sexuality; he created us male and female. This gift can be used—and misused, as it often is. To understand it and share in its joy and to help others do the same, Christians will have to start from where they are, share what they know to be true, and rise above their opinions in the search for sexual integrity.

QUESTIONS FOR DISCUSSION

1. Is there more freedom today in terms of openness about sex? Can you talk with your children openly about it? Is there more or less of a "generation gap" now than say, ten years ago? Would you say that teen-agers today are knowledgeable about sex?

2. One newspaper editor made these comments about the Second North American Conference on Church and Family in Hamilton, Ontario, in 1966:

"There is little doubt that many of the old rules have become indefensible. Often in the past our society has put chastity before charity; often the church's rigorous concept of morality has thrown out compassion and understanding. But the answer to this is not a contorted bending over backwards by the church, which at times has the appearance of being excruciatingly anxious to be tolerant. Behavior which, at one time, would have brought down the wrath of the church on the offender, is now just excused but presented almost as if it were a worthy objective of a properly reorientated religious outlook. This can hardly fail to perplex the younger generation which stands in need of guidance."

Do you think that the new breed has been bending over backwards on this issue?

3. "There is nothing to be ashamed of in enjoying your food: there would be everything to be ashamed of if half the world made food the main interest of their lives and spent their time looking at pictures of food and dribbling and smacking their lips. . . . You can get a large audience together for a strip-tease act—that is, to watch a girl undress on the stage. Now suppose you came to a country where you could fill a theatre by simply bringing a covered plate on to the stage and then slowly lifting the cover so as to let everyone see, just before the lights went out, that it contained a mutton chop or a bit of bacon, would you not think that in that country something had gone wrong with the appetite for food? And would not anyone who had grown up in a different world think there was something equally queer about the state of the sex instinct among us?" [2]

[2] C. S. Lewis, *Mere Christianity* (New York: The Macmillan Co., 1958), pp. 77, 75.

Do you think that sex is out of perspective as Lewis suggests? What does it mean to take sex more seriously or less seriously than we ought?

4.   "There is the temptation to condone the frivolous or superficial sexual encounter on the grounds that no one was hurt. This temptation is full of dangers. One is simply that people cannot tell beforehand what feelings will be aroused by a relationship. Anyone who has tried to reason himself out of feelings of jealousy or injured self-esteem knows what I mean. But even if it were true that two people can pass through so intimate an experience and come out untouched, is that cause for congratulation? The Old Testament speaks of sex as carnal knowledge, and that is a very significant insight. It is an encounter in which we know and are known intimately, in the secret places of our souls. 'After such knowledge, what forgiveness?' asks T. S. Eliot. What is worse than to be known fully but not loved? We cannot forgive the person who has gained such knowledge of us but whose knowledge is unleavened by affection and caring. Neither can we forgive the person whom we know intimately but do not love." [3]

What does Dr. Lacey mean when he says "we cannot forgive the person whom we know intimately but do not love"? Is a sexual experience in which "no one was hurt" worth having? Do men and women differ in their attitudes toward sexual relationships? In what ways?

5. *"Playboy* tries to give the American male an identity and the right frame of reference. So if you spend the bachelor years doing what *Playboy* suggests, you wind up

[3] Paul A. Lacey, "Temptation—A Meditation on Sexual Morality," *Pendle Hill Bulletin* No. 170, April, 1964, p. 6.

with a happier, more stable marriage." [4] Do you agree that premarital sexual experiences and a few years of "seeking after pleasure" will better prepare a man for a "happier, more stable marriage"? Why? Why not?

6. What does it mean to be "really honest" about sexual relationships? How can you be really honest before the relationship has taken place? What if you thought you were really honest with a girl (i.e, you told her you loved her), and after a sexual experience with her, you discovered you don't really love her?

7. Consider the following Commandments:
   a. Honor your father and your mother.
   b. You shall not kill.
   c. You shall not commit adultery.
   d. You shall not steal.
   e. You shall not bear false witness against your neighbor.
   f. You shall not covet your neighbor's house; you shall not covet your neighbor's wife, or his manservant, or his maidservant, or his ox, or his ass, or anything that is your neighbor's.

Which of the above Commandments ought never to be broken? Are there any circumstances under which it is "right" to kill, steal, lie, or commit adultery? To what extent does one's moral action depend upon the circumstances? Are the Commandments general guidelines or inflexible commands?

8. Joseph Fletcher tells of this case from World War II. A German woman was captured by the Russians and taken to a P.O.W. Camp. The only way for her to gain release from the Camp and be returned to her family

---

[4] Hugh Hefner, "An Empire Built on Sex," *Life,* October 29, 1965, p. 68b.

(where she was sorely needed) was through serious illness or pregnancy. She decided to ask the guard to impregnate her, which he did. Her condition being medically verified, she was sent back to her family in Berlin. They welcomed her with open arms, even when she told them how she managed her release. Did she do the right and "Christian" thing?

9. Should the churches take a firmer stand on their relationship to marriage, e.g., should ministers refuse to marry couples without counseling? Should it take a less firm stand on marital (and sexual) problems, such as divorce, homosexuality, and premarital intercourse? What is the stand of your church on these issues?

10. How should we instruct our children about sexual relationships? Should we advocate virginity? Virginity until the engagement period? Experimentation? What would a new Christian sexual code be, were you to write one?

11. Lester Kirkendall, an authority in sex education, says that satisfying personal relationships must include the following, insofar as sex is involved.

- a. Adherence to a value system which makes a concern for the improvement of interpersonal relations a paramount value.
- b. Acceptance of the fact that the sexual impulse is essentially positive and life-giving in nature. Rather than fearing it, our task is learning how to direct and utilize it.
- c. Much discussion and objective consideration of the nature of sex, and its place in relationships. These discussions need to cut across age and sex lines, and to be approached in the same manner as we approach discussions on other subjects.
- d. Scrupulous care to avoid exploitive, self-centered use of sex.

    e. Much attention to ways in which satisfying and complementing sex roles can be developed.

    f. The release of pressures and the elimination of commercial uses which attach extraneous values to sex.[5]

Do these standards, in your opinion, deny premarital sexual relationships? Do they encourage them? How can we best avoid "exploitive, self-centered use of sex"?

BIBLIOGRAPHY

Fletcher, Joseph. *Situation Ethics: The New Morality.* Philadelphia: Westminster Press, 1966.

Hettlinger, Richard F. *Living with Sex: The Student's Dilemma.* New York: Seabury Press, 1966.

Kirkendall, Lester A. *Premarital Intercourse and Interpersonal Relationships.* New York: Julian Press, 1961.

Pike, James A. *You and the New Morality.* New York: Harper & Row, 1967.

Trobisch, Walter. *I Loved a Girl.* New York: Harper & Row, 1965.

[5] *Premarital Intercourse and Interpersonal Relationships,* p. 252.

chapter four

A FRESH UNDERSTANDING OF GOD

The people who have caused traditions to be shaken at their very foundations have been the radical theologians among the new breed. Most people in most traditional churches don't really worry much about theology, even though nearly everyone has some kind of theological system; but when a few scholars are written up by *Time* magazine as having said that "God is dead," confusion and chaos take over. Actually, this theological ferment is simply the latest in a series of analyses and criticisms of the "foundations" of Christianity. Many ministers wouldn't dare explain form criticism of the Bible to their church members, even though it has been standard teaching in most first-rate seminaries for a long time. Many ministers, who would not even regard themselves as members of the new breed, would be hard pressed to defend a belief in the virgin birth or other "fundamentals" of the Christian faith, which thousands of conservative members take for granted.

Nevertheless, this kind of analysis and criticism has shaken the foundations. Even a scholar such as J. B. Phillips has expressed his deep concern in one of his most recent books, *The Ring of Truth*. Phillips says in his opening remarks:

For twenty-five years I have written for the ordinary man who is no theologian. Alas, today, he frequently gets the impression that the New Testament is no longer historically reliable.

What triggered off my anger (righteous, I trust) against some of our "experts" is this. A clergyman, old, retired, useless if you like, took his own life because his reading of the "new theology," and even some programs on television, finally drove him, in his loneliness and ill-health, to conclude that his own life's work had been founded upon a lie. He felt that these highly qualified writers and speakers must know so much more than he that they must be right. Jesus Christ did not really rise from the dead and the New Testament, on which he had based his life and ministry, was no more than a bundle of myths.[1]

The fact that the "death of God" received so much publicity is its primary significance. As a theological idea it probably would have died a natural death, as it did in its intellectual form shortly after the time of Nietzsche. But it was news, shocking news, to the Christian on the street. And when that Christian and his parents heard the news, they were disturbed. They

[1] (New York: The Macmillan Co., 1967), p. 9.

were especially shaken when they learned that the three main spokesmen for the movement were teachers in reputable seminaries. What, after all, were the world and the church coming to?

Exactly what these theologians were saying has never been made completely clear, to this writer or perhaps to themselves. The main force that kept their ideas alive was the reaction against them. Some reactions were predictable! "I know God is alive; I spoke to Him this morning." "Our God is not only alive; he hasn't even been sick." It is significant that their ideas about the death of God never really gained widespread acceptance among theologians, and most of the commentaries about the varying beliefs of the death of God are semisociological. They are efforts to find out what really was "bugging" these theologians.

Persons who feel, however, that these ideas were simply thoughts in passing, which had few implications and few serious consequences, may also be mistaken. There is no question but that the death-of-God conversation has caused confusion and has led to some bad results. A lot of people who had already rejected the church now were able to find reasons for having done so. Some who heard that God was dead were able to say triumphantly, "I told you so a long time ago." Probably, too, some sincere seekers after God became discouraged and gave up the search. Those people whose religious lives are centered primarily around the seminary or the college are probably basically unaware of what such ideas as these do to the seeker in a local church somewhere, whose mind is not theologically oriented and whose religious experience may have been limited. Thus we must say that the radical

76

theology of our time is important, not so much for the value of its ideas, but because of public response and reaction to them.

Yet, having been honest about the dangers and realistic about the effects of radical theology, we find it also important to say that such thinking is a sign of our times. It is one of the calling cards of the new breed of Christian that no idea be left uncriticized and no person who seeks to make religion relevant to his time be denied the opportunity to take himself where his ideas lead him. It may be that we will profit more in the long run from this openness than we have suffered from it. It may be that by asking the basic questions once again, as men before us have done, we will revitalize theology, and Christian experience will play a larger place in thinking about God than it has for centuries.

For too long we have assumed that God had a role in things without really discovering for ourselves the relationship of God to our lives. The persons who represent establishment Christianity may have, at other times and in other ways, experienced the reality of God in their lives, but they dare not make the mistake of assuming that a new generation of Christians will experience him in the same way. Because this generation may not be able to experience God in the same way, they will have to ask the hard questions and come to some conclusions—hopefully, temporary ones— which may seem to deny the reality of God.

We must take seriously the fact that to neutral observers God has disappeared from the scene of contemporary society. In the past we looked for signs of God in the way people acted when they talked about him. Now signs of God are not so apparent. People, by and large, do not gather together in great congregations regularly, Sunday after Sunday, to sing his praises and listen to his word. People, on the whole, do not say their prayers regularly at night—or in the morning, for that matter—and if they do, they are prepared to take a considerable amount of ridicule for doing so. Our holidays are no longer holy days. Good Friday is more and more like every other Friday for most people. In many cities Good Friday is now a holiday, and the largest industries and businesses will close in recognition of the day. However, attendance at good Friday services has been no higher and, in many cases, has been lower than when men were working at their regular jobs. Christmas, we all know, is more and more like any other winter carnival. Roman Catholics don't have to eat fish on Friday anymore, and they are not going to confession the way they used to. God has by and large disappeared from the contemporary scene. There are many people, especially in our large cities, who have never even heard the Gospel of Christ preached—in its new or old forms.

I can remember one experience when I was working on night duty in a detention home for juvenile delinquents. Part of the responsibility of the job included the sharing of the evening meal with the teen-age boys who were being held at this temporary home before going to trial. On one occasion a boy, who was sixteen years of age, was included in the group for dinner, and when we bowed our heads for a blessing, he had no idea of what we were doing. For all he knew, "grace" was somebody's sister. The signs of God's presence had been left out of his life, and even the traditional ones were foreign to him.

Nor can a neutral observer see God reflected in the way people think. When a hurricane or flood wipes out a whole village, not many people think that God sent it. They think that it was a natural disturbance in the elements that in most cases could be predicted and its course plotted. When a nation wins or loses a war, not many people think that God led them to victory or punished them by defeat. They won or lost because they did or did not have the weapons and the will to win. When people do something outrageous, we normally blame the way they were brought up. When we study the course of human history, we see no trace of anything but human factors—conflict growing out of human desire for land, or raw materials, or for status in the world. To this extent, it is fair to say that there is some truth in the report that God is dead: He seemingly has disappeared from the scene of our actions and our thinking. In such a world as this, is it really any surprise that a theology will appear which uses as its keynote the idea that God is dead?

Such a world as this has also had a positive effect on our theological understandings. Theology today has become *humanistic* in a new and vital sense. We have come to think about the action of God in the world in ways that do not keep him removed from it. We are told to "humanize" the institutions of our society. We turn to Bonhoeffer—at least the new breed does—and are told that Jesus was "the man for others." We are told that "man has come of age." We are confronted with sermons and articles again and again which make the point that Christ died for the *world,* not the church, and the world has become the great arena in which the Christian is to live the life of holy obedience.

Notice what is different about this: the new breed does not speak of "God out there." The idea of a God who is like the genial grandfather with a long white beard, who soothes small children and flatters old ladies, is dead. This is expressed not only in theology but in the stuff of modern piety. Malcolm Boyd, in the introduction to his book of prayers, which is called *Are You Running with Me, Jesus?*, says this about the nature of prayer:

Prayer could no longer be offered to God *up there* but to God *here;* prayer had to be natural and real, not phony or contrived; it was not about *other things* . . . but *these* things, however unattractive, jarring or even socially outcast they might be.

God, I discovered, was not an upper-middle-class snob in private, clublike "holy of holies" nor was he an impersonal I.B.M. machine computing petty sins in some celestial office building above the clouds.[2]

In other words, to this outspoken member of the new breed God is down here with us, participating in this stinking, wonderful world, and all of a sudden a lot of people who had crossed God off have begun to take him seriously.

A second result of this turmoil has been the blurring of the gap between the sacred and the secular. For years we have been treating life much in the way that *Time* magazine treats it—by putting it into compartments. If you take a group of four-year-olds and teach them to

[2] Pp. 12-13.

relate nicely to each other around the sandbox in the name of a nursery school association, that is sweet but very secular. However, if you do it on Sunday morning, it is not only nice but Christian. If you go to Africa to teach mathematics to the natives for the Peace Corps, this is a good but secular deed. If, however, you teach mathematics in the same way from the same textbook in a school sponsored by the Methodists or the Baptists, you have become a missionary. If you chaperone a hayride for the 4-H Club of your town, this is probably risky. However, if you do it for the youth fellowship of your church, it is not only risky but Christian.

In these times, as we can see, this dichotomy is breaking down. Now there are many people who are saying that God is interested in man and in the world, who seek to serve him in ways that have been regarded heretofore as secular. Now we find churches involved in political work among slum people. Many ministers of the new breed will be lining up voters for registration in the south. On a college campus many among the most committed students may be cool toward the traditional church, but they will put in many hours tutoring disadvantaged children from the slums. And, they say, they regard this as a "religious" expression of themselves. Many among the new breed will say that in several instances the secular agency does a more effective humanitarian work and more clearly represents the will of God in action than does the so-called religious agency in the name of the church.

The other side of the coin, however, is equally fascinating. Those churches which encourage their people to get out into the secular world and serve God are finding these members looking to the church for fellowship and inspiration in a way that they never did before. The more people work in the world, the more they need the church for strength and help. Their need is having a radical effect on what goes on in our churches. Forms of worship and meditation are being seriously affected. People who want help and strength directly from God and are unable to find it in the traditional language and traditional forms are developing new language and new forms. As people did many years ago when they wrote *their* hymns and *their* prayers, a new generation of Christians is seeking to express its beliefs about God and its experience of God in an idiom that is familiar and real to them.

Thus, to a greater degree than ever before, Christians are experimenting with worship. We find persons using jazz in place of the good old gospel hymns when they sing praises to God. We find them expressing themselves in words that another generation might have thought blasphemous when used in talking about God. We find them relating their experiences to God in ways that are meaningful to them. Thus few prayers given by the new breed talk about sheep and shepherds, but many prayers talk about man and his loneliness. In keeping with the blurring of the distinction between the sacred and the secular, as persons look for new ways of expressing their faith and their search for meaning, they may turn to what heretofore would have been regarded as very unlikely sources of inspiration. An article in *Renewal Magazine* by Stephen C. Rose, one of the leaders among the new breed of Christian, is entitled "Bob Dylan As Theologian." [3] Bob

[3] October-November, 1965, p. 5.

Dylan is a folk singer, who came out of the midwest by way of New York's Greenwich Village into the minds and hearts of countless young people and adults.

It is not uncommon in a worship service on a college campus for the student congregation to sing one of Bob Dylan's songs in place of a traditional hymn. It is not uncommon to hear them singing in reverence and in awe his "Blowing in the Wind." It is not uncommon, because some of the words ask the *relevant* question. "And how many times must cannonballs fly, before they are forever banned?"

Or the new breed may look more carefully at a song by the Beatles, such as "Eleanor Rigby," than they do at the tracts put out by the department of evangelism. They may look at such a song carefully because it speaks of the loneliness and the estrangement of many people who represent experiences with which they are familiar better than do hymns from another age. Would you believe that the Beatles may know more about the nature of loneliness than John Jones, the local pastor?

The attitude toward worship of many such Christians is illustrated pointedly by this letter to the editor in *The Christian Century:*

At the Presbyterian Center here we have been wrestling with the problem of worship, trying to discover why most of us either laugh or cry through the typical morning worship service. At last someone has put my feeling into words. . . . Somehow the church has got to realize that words no longer effectively communicate to our generation. As I write this I am listening to the theme from *Alfie.* Just a minute ago the record was the theme from *Georgie Girl.* These two films caused more thinking on my part, depicted more of reality to me, than all of the sermons I have listened to in my 20 years, and I doubt if I am alone. The church has lost my generation—even those of us who still attend regularly, are committed to her, have decided to "stay in." We are bored with her services and with our fumbling attempts at "liturgical renewal." I am convinced that movies are the way to communicate reality. The *visual,* not the oral, is the direction the church must follow.[5]

The result of this thrust is that some relevant and moving jazz liturgies, modern songs, and Christian tools of worship are being developed. It is also true that a lot of shallow, superficial, and worthless material is being tossed about in worship services by many people who are hooked on faddism rather than serious worship. This, however, is the price that must be paid as men seek to answer the question, "What does God have to do with life?" Whenever such questions are asked and taken seriously, we get both good and bad results. This is simply one more reason why the traditional church and its established congregations must share in the search together, to see what the experiences of today's world have to say to a new generation of Christians. And dialogue about worship will offer help and guidance in sorting out what is good and what is bad from the results of this search.

The third new thing that is happening as men seek a fresh understanding of God is the stress on the ecumenical movement. While it is true that the ecumenical movement has been off the ground and flying for

[5] Paul E. Thomason, in a letter to the editor. Copyright 1968 Christian Century Foundation. Reprinted by permission from the April 17, 1968 issue of *The Christian Century.*

many years, never before in our history has there been as much interdenominational and even interreligious dialogue as is now the case. The new breed is caught up in cooperative Christianity. The day may well be passed when a strictly denominational appeal can be made to them. The little questions about God, which, unfortunately, many denominations have stressed more than the big questions, are of little importance to them. There is a mood of trust and sincerity which is enabling Christians who are of good will to sit side by side and to agree and disagree in love.

This mood is reflected in a cartoon which appeared one time in a national magazine. The cartoon showed a group of natives dressed in loincloths, gathered in front of an enormous idol which had horns and several arms and a great, vicious mouth with huge teeth. The spokesman for the group of natives standing in front of it said, according to the caption below the cartoon: "Oh, great fish god, devourer of our enemies, bringer of rain, and mother of the sun, we humbly beg thy leave to go join the Methodists."

This mood pervades the church today, and it means that men are getting down to brass tacks about religion. Pope John gave the ecumenical movement an enormous impetus during his brief time in the Vatican, and the Catholic Church has made strides toward Protestantism that have frightened even many Protestants. It has a momentum that will not now be stopped. This again is new and fresh. It is so new and so fresh that we may forget that even ten years ago many of the things that we are now calmly discussing and planning to do in a cooperative way as Christians were unthinkable. In one of the most dramatic ecumenical movements yet the Roman Catholic Church's Woodstock College voted to move from its wooded Maryland retreat near Baltimore to the urban environs of New Haven, Connecticut. The Catholic Seminary plans to affiliate with Yale University's predominantly Protestant divinity school. If the move receives final approval from Rome, it will bring together some of the nations' most prominent Catholic and Protestant theologians. The reason for this radical move? To inject Woodstock into a more urban environment, to break theology's intellectual isolation from other academic areas, and to bring Catholics into closer contact with other Christian traditions.

This has been especially shocking to many among the Christian faith who for years have been suspicious of Roman Catholics and Romanism. There are many Protestants who have been brought up to be fearful of the mysterious Roman Church around the corner from them and of those large Catholic families, which soon could dominate a political structure or overpopulate the school district. Many Protestants revealed their prejudices as they talked about Christians "and Catholics." The new breed has reopened questions about this kind of relationship, and they are approaching it more as brothers than as natural enemies. Christians within Protestantism are cooperating to a greater degree than ever before, too, and forms and structures of religious worship are being modified because differences are being played down.

A fourth result of our religious turmoil is that the new breed is stressing a new sense of *vocation*. There is one phrase that is heard again and again among the dynamic Christians who are products of this time.

It is the phrase "the church in mission." So long as you have God up in the sky, so long as you separate the sacred and the secular along rigid lines, so long as you need experts who represent the provincialism of one religious sect over another—then we have a church dominated by professional clergymen. Now, however, there is great evidence that we are going forward by going backward—back to a biblical understanding of what vocation is, and means.

There should be no misunderstanding about this point: there is a desperate need for more pastors, missionaries, priests, and other religious professionals. We are in serious condition now in terms of our leadership needs. But one of the reasons we are shorthanded is a good reason: men and women are consciously declaring themselves for vocations that *become* Christian because these people *make* them Christian. One seminary—and its experience has been matched by many others—is finding that more people than ever before are wanting to come to the seminary for a year or two before they go back to their normal vocations of high school teaching, social work, being a housewife, or the world of business. They have a sense of vocation which says that they need to develop spiritual understanding and gain theological competence as well as to develop the special skills needed to do their special jobs.

A recent article in the *National Observer* showed that while seminaries are finding themselves shorthanded in their search for faculty and students, undergraduate schools have more religion courses than ever before, and some of the best teachers are ending up there rather than in the first-rate seminaries. Unfortunately, the professional religious ministry is losing people, but the good news is that the dedicated person is seeing his job as a vocation—a Christian vocation. If this be true, it is progress. One of the battles which continue to be fought in the established and traditional ministry of today is the stereotype problem—the rigid and clear-cut separation between clergy and laity. For years, for example, it has been assumed that only ministers can pray. They have been called to many meetings, banquets, and other occasions for the single purpose of giving the invocation or the benediction. Some of their experiences have been bizarre, to say the least. It is not uncommon for a minister to be asked to such diverse places as the opening game of Little League or a horse show in order to give an invocation. Fortunately, thank God, we are moving away from this kind of understanding of Christian vocation and ministry. The barrier has been broken down, and the priesthood of all believers, for the new breed, is becoming a reality. Many among the new breed in the parish ministry are taking their new roles seriously. The meaning of "vocation" has changed for them, as well as for the Christian who is a schoolteacher or butcher or businessman. It is not uncommon to pick up a newspaper or other periodical and find an article about this minister or that whose ministry is becoming mission in the world.

Even the ministry to suburbia is beginning to face realistically the special problems of the affluent and their personal temptations. One Presbyterian synod sent a minister to a suburban county where there was no church. His purpose, as has often been the case, was to organize a church in the suburbs. However, in the process of conducting his business from rented space, he has found a different kind of involvement in the life of this suburban area. In a newspaper interview, he made these comments about life in suburbia,

When I came here, I was told by another minister friend that all they cared about out there is their kids and the grass. And I thought he was crazy, but I'm afraid in some ways I have to agree with him. It seems to me that I can even tell something about how narrow a person's mind is by how narrow his grass is; that a person of broad interests and broad mind doesn't have the time to cultivate extremely narrow grass. This means you can drive down the street and get ideas of the kind of families that you are dealing with by the condition of their grass. Now, of course, this isn't completely true but it does tend to sum up the extremely introverted interests and concerns of so many families. I often drive by these areas with my top down in my convertible, and they know me. I'll wave to them and they just stare back like they are in a trance. This is quite upsetting—this ruthless sense of loneliness which I know so many are sharing. You take this kind of family which is simply pervading suburbia and you find a real concern in trying to minister to them, trying to help them out of their loneliness and apathy to involvement in the world.

Ministers such as these are part of the new breed who are finding involvement in mission, even among the affluent in suburbia.

Christians in many areas of life, especially those who view life itself as a sacrament, are looking for new ways of expressing this belief. The new breed, and many traditional Christians as well, are looking for ways within the common ventures of life by which they can, and ought to, experience the living Christ.

Many young Christian parents, for example, are attracted to the idea that mealtime can be a communion experience. New-breed Christians are not bent on rejecting the rituals of the church; in fact, in many quarters movement back to liturgy and stress upon the sacraments are gaining favor. However, new-breed Christians are trying to see relationships in life as sacramental experiences. They are thinking of the pressures of life, which require Christian responses, as the "baptism of fire." These can have sacramental value. The number of holy days may increase, or at least change, as Christian parents make high and holy occasions of days in their family life which ought to have a religious dimension in their interpretation. The first day that a child goes to school, the first date for the young person, the wedding anniversary, and other special occasions within a family—these events can be interpreted from a sacramental point of view, and this understanding of life *as vocation* is progress.

Such an attitude was demonstrated by one family which, because of the martyrdom of the husband, received a great deal of national publicity. Bruce Klunder was a handsome twenty-six-year-old Presbyterian minister who was killed in a civil rights demonstration in the Cleveland area. One article about the courageous way in which his wife responded to this tragedy included this quotation from Joan Klunder:

Religion as ritual was never any particularly large part of our lives—we never made much fuss about family prayer sessions or things like that—and Bruce was basically a quiet person. He wasn't the wild eyed radical or some kind of nut. The night before his death we were talking about an accusation that whites were doing too much in the Civil Rights movement. He said, one can never apologize for doing too much—only for doing too little.[6]

How parents who are Christian approach their religion in this day may be different from the way in which parents two generations ago approached religion. There may be less stress on formal and ritualistic expressions of Christianity and a greater stress upon the need to be loyal to Christ in the world.

A new interpretation of stewardship is taking place, too, and this will have serious implications for the local church. The stewardship of money may include, not just giving to a local church which may use those gifts to buy better curtains for their kitchen, but the effort to *raise taxes* to improve education for ghetto children. It may include petitioning to increase the portion of money that goes for persons who will benefit from the war on poverty or Operation Head Start or Upward Bound. It may even be said that it is a form of stewardship when a person uses his money to set himself free to be a better parent, a better citizen, and a better human being.

Joseph C. Fletcher argues that . . . Christian stewardship must keep pace with the increasing organization of modern society, [in] that it applies to such areas as smoke abatement, urban renewal, education and delinquency. . . .

Joseph C. McLelland argues for "corporate stewardship," not only in churches but also in larger social groupings. He advocates a thorough understanding of an appreciation

[6] B. and C. Remsberg, "What Four Brave Women Told Their Children," *Good Housekeeping,* May, 1967, p. 152.

for social power; he suggests that corporate stewardship means group responsibility in the use of that power.[7]

Just as there are dangers in making religion consist primarily of ritual and separation from life—the danger which "old-breed" Christians have had to face—there are dangers also in taking this new sacramental view of life. It is at this point that new-breed Christians need to listen carefully to what traditionalists have to say. There is danger in too easy an identification, as people may start saying that all things are Christian. They may regard the secular city as good just because it's there. Some mealtimes are *not* communion. Some experiences and pressures of life do not cause persons to change their orientation in a way which later could be identified as "baptismal." People can merely use special days to justify their selfishness, instead of using them for experiences with a Christian dimension. Stewardship of money can come to be a kind of right-wing rejection of giving to the church at all, not just an effort to use tax money as a modern form of Christian stewardship. In other words, the new danger is one of rationalization, as people can use the idea of a sacramental view of life to justify that which they want to do anyway.

Once again, the need for Christians to discuss such matters as these in our day is vital. We need both the discipline of formal worship *and* the sacramental view of life, which will give all of life meaning. Which comes first, we do not know. We only know that the persons who will be able to get most out of their formal reli-

[7] Quoted by William H. Jennings, "Stewardship and Social Action," *The Christian Century,* December 13, 1967, p. 1595.

gious expressions will be the people who are able also to view life as an opportunity to experience God.

The God who lives in the world and can be experienced day by day is the living God. Christians of this generation who are part of today's world want to experience God in ways that are meaningful and real to them. Persons from another generation who have found vital experiences of him in the past must be not only willing to tolerate this, but they need to participate with the new breed in their search. Two or three, gathered together, still promote optimum conditions for the presence of the Holy Spirit to be felt. It is nearly impossible to experience God consistently by oneself. One must have the shared experience of other people with their particular and special emphases and ideas. God continues to make himself known to us day by day, as he has done through the centuries. He continues to make himself known to us through people and events, and if we will speak with one another about it, perhaps we will have the eyes to see, the ears to hear, and the hearts to feel his presence. We may even discover we are seeking the same God, the One who revealed himself in Jesus Christ.

QUESTIONS FOR DISCUSSION

1. Do you agree with the observation on page 77 that "God has disappeared from the scene of contemporary society"?

If so, why has this happened? Was it because of the "forces of evil"? Has the established church failed? Is it because the church has not kept up with the times in its ideas and forms? If you disagree with the statement, what popular signs of belief in God exist? Church attendance? Church buildings? The status of ministers in the community?

2. Read Malcolm Boyd's statement about prayer on page 80. Does this seem to make prayer seem commonplace and "less sacred"? Consider the following prayer from his book *Are You Running with Me, Jesus?*

"It's morning, Jesus. It's morning, and here's the light and sound all over again

I've got to move fast . . . get into the bathroom, wash up, grab a bite to eat, and run some more.

I just don't feel like it, Lord. What I really want to do is get back into bed, pull up the covers, and sleep. All I seem to want today is the big sleep, and here I've got to run all over again.

Where am I running? You know these things I can't understand. It's not that I need to have you tell me. What counts most is just that somebody knows, and it's you. That helps a lot.

So I'll follow along, okay? But lead, Lord. Now I've got to run. Are you running with me, Jesus?"[8]

Does this seem like a prayer to you? Compare it to the following traditional prayer, often used in worship services:

"O God, who art real to those who come to thee in trust; increase our faith, that feeling toward thee as children, we may trust where we cannot see, and hope where all seems doubtful, ever looking to thee as our Father that ordereth all things well, and patiently doing the work thou hast given us to do: according to the word of thy Son Jesus Christ."

3. What determines the appropriateness of a song for use in worship? Is "The Battle Hymn of the Republic" more

[8] From *Are You Running with Me, Jesus?* by Malcolm Boyd. Copyright © 1965 by Malcolm Boyd. Reprinted by permission of Holt, Rinehart and Winston, Inc.

appropriate than, say "Blowing in the Wind" by Bob Dylan? What standards should be used in making such judgments?

4. One critic has said that much of the popular music with religious overtones which catches the fancy of the new breed merely states the problem without offering the hope which ought to characterize the "good news" of the gospel. Do you agree? Are there any contemporary songs with religious overtones which do demonstrate the mood of joy and triumph that Christians feel ought to characterize the gospel?

5. See the movie *Alfie* if possible. Why would the young Presbyterian who wrote the letter on page 83 say that this film "caused more thinking and depicted more of reality . . . than all of the sermons he'd ever heard"? To what extent do hymns, sermons, and traditional prayers labor under the handicap of overfamiliarity?

6. Read the Apostles' Creed. "I believe in God the Father Almighty, maker of heaven and earth;

And in Jesus Christ his only Son, our Lord: Who was conceived by the Holy Ghost, Born of the Virgin Mary: Suffered under Pontius Pilate, Was crucified, dead, and buried: He descended into hell; The third day he arose again from the dead: He ascended into heaven, And sitteth on the right hand of God the Father Almighty: From thence he shall come to judge the quick and the dead.

I believe in the Holy Ghost: The Holy Catholic Church; The Communion of Saints: The Forgiveness of sins: The Resurrection of the body: and the Life everlasting."

What does it mean to say that Christ "descended into hell"? What does it mean that he "sitteth on the right hand of God"? Who are "the quick and the dead"? What is the "Communion of Saints"? Are these terms which are clear and meaningful to Christians today? Are they misleading?

7. Does your church have continual and significant relationships with Roman Catholics? How has your attitude toward Catholics been affected by the recent conversations about ecumenicity? Do you think differences between Roman Catholics and Protestants should be played down, or will something valuable in the Christian faith be lost if the differences are not faced frankly? What can be lost? What can be gained?

8. Is it possible to have family worship in this mobile age? In what ways can families stress the sacramental view of life, if "religion as ritual" plays a smaller part? (See page 90.)

BIBLIOGRAPHY

Boyd, Malcolm. *Are You Running with Me, Jesus?* New York: Holt, Rinehart & Winston, 1965.

Quoist, Michel. *Prayers.* New York: Sheed & Ward, 1963.

Raines, Robert A. *Creative Brooding.* New York: The Macmillan Co., 1966.

Robinson, John A. T. *The New Reformation?* Philadelphia: Westminster Press, 1965.

Trueblood, D. Elton. *The Incendiary Fellowship.* New York: Harper & Row, 1967.

chapter five

MEANWHILE, BACK AT THE CHURCH

Much—perhaps too much—has already been written about the renewal of the parish church. Articles on the subject have appeared in most Christian journals and even in several popular magazines. Of the writing of books on church renewal, there seems to be no end. It would be inaccurate, however, to say that the books and the articles merely repeat one another, for they do not. They range from reluctant pessimism about the local church to passionate optimism about its future. The new breed of Christian often says that the local church, per se, has no future—and only an insignificant present—or he calls for and prescribes health plans for the sick churches that are scattered across the land.

We must face the fact that new breed and the local church many times seem to be working in different ways, toward different goals, and with different understanding of what the proper business of the church ought to be. The heartbeat of the historical church has always been local congregations, but the church has had many different forms. The forces of renewal will begin in the local church, and this is the important fact that must be kept in mind. To ask what can be saved out of the church, as it is, and what should be changed is to ask the wrong kind of question. A better question, says Joseph Mathews, a radical Christian if ever there were one, is: "What doth the Lord require of us?" Mathews says this:

As for the institutional church, all of it can go if none of it serves today's needs. The only things that need to be conserved are the things that can be used. If the women's society or men's club is the useful tool, then use it. If it isn't, let it die. If preaching is still a tool of being radically obedient, use it. If not, abandon it. Today, any lucid person in Jesus Christ understands there are two alternatives relative to renewal of the Church. One is that the church has been said "No" to by God. Therefore, the awakened man of faith must operate outside the institutional structures of the past, creating the new forms, new structures. Several leaders have chosen that alternative. The other alternative is to believe that the church is renewable from within, and this on several levels. But what is renewed is renewed, a metamorphosis shall have taken place. We at the Ecumenical Institute are fanatics at the point that the church is renewable from within.[1]

What Colin Williams and Joseph Mathews and other radical transformers of the local parish have in mind is

[1] "On Church Renewal," *Together,* March, 1966, p. 49.

something with which the new breed will certainly be sympathetic. It is of their warp and woof to believe that the local congregation can be changed, must be changed, and will be changed before they will be able conscientiously to participate in it.

The problem continues to plague us, however, as to what to do in the meantime. Undoubtedly, local congregations fifty years from now in almost every community in America will be considerably different from what they are now. Their programs will be different, their membership will be different, and the way in which they seek to serve the world will be different. Our immediate problem, though, is to make it possible for such a transition to be orderly and useful in this interim period. What can the local church, as it is now established, do to get its creative, young, and vital Christians working in cooperation with itself? What will be the ways in which the new breed will open itself to the ideas and thinking of the local church, much of which is sound and useful, albeit conservative, that will enable them to cooperate in fighting the world's battles rather than fighting with each other?

To be honest, it is necessary to say that some churches are so inflexible in their program and attitudes that the radical Christian may not be able to bridge the dialogue gap. It is also accurate to say that some among the so-called liberal and progressive new breed have closed their minds to the established church and demonstrate every bit as much rigidity as the congregations they condemn. It is easy to be critical of each side's ideas and opinions, as we are always found wanting whenever we compare ourselves to the high standards of the New Testament or God's intention for his church.

Nevertheless, if local churches are to face the future realistically, and if the new breed is to have a lump to leaven, concrete, down-to-earth efforts will have to be made in which Christians of many varieties can participate. This will surely be more helpful than either praising or burying the church in its present form.

THE COMMUNITY OF WORSHIP

When genuine worship, i.e., spiritual communion with God, is achieved by a congregation, many other problems can then be handled. Christians of many points of view want—indeed long for—the experience of worship. In this interim period, local churches will have to provide more than one kind of worship experience at more than one time of day on more days than Sunday. If a dialogue between traditional and radical Christians teaches us anything, it clearly shows that some forms, words, symbols, and structures communicate with some Christians better than others. Worship takes place (or fails to occur) in the minds and hearts of those present. It has some objective elements which do not depend on the subjective reactions of those present, but Protestant worship seldom needs justification if worshipers are consistently experiencing communion with God.

Thus, in addition to the "regular 11:00 A.M. service," a local church could have another regular hour of worship which is gauged to the needs of the new breed. The pastor and/or official board could invite some of the Christians who are dissatisfied with traditional worship to share in the planning and leadership of the worship period. This could be a time for jazz liturgies, dialogue sermons, folk masses, unprogrammed or silent worship, dramatic productions, or even modern dance. Many a clergyman among the new breed would love to have a place and time for experimentation with worship. Occasionally, or gradually, elements of tradition would be introduced in the "experimental" hour just as innovation could be added to the regular routine. Whenever possible, persons who claim to be helped by one kind of service or the other should have opportunity to discuss their experiences with each other. Even if minds are not open, such a dialogue will enable persons to know better what worship is and ought to be.

Christians and would-be Christians many times respond in surprising ways to innovation and/or tradition. Students in one college, for example, were deeply moved by a jazz liturgy which was performed by choir and ensemble. Some had tears in their eyes, and many verbally expressed appreciation for what was to them a genuine religious experience. Ironically, many at the same time probably were unaware that the liturgy which was both read and sung was simply a restatement of ancient traditional creeds, including a musical version of the Apostles' Creed. The lesson we can learn from this experience is that communication of traditional ideas is often what is at stake, not a rejection of Christ-centered worship.

The time and place of worship can be modified during this interim period, too. Sunday evening services, of any kind, may be difficult to revive in today's fast-moving world, but worship at other times may be experimented with instead. At a recent Disciples of Christ conference, delegates weighed seriously the suggestion of "moving" Sunday morning to Thursday night. In other words, worship services and Sunday school would take place on Thursday evening, thereby leaving the entire weekend free for family activities. This kind of adjustment, of course, is not a problem of scheduling so much as it is a problem of psychologically shifting gears. Could Christians come to think of Thursday evening services as real worship?

One Ohio church, recently formed, meets only one Sunday per month as a group. This is an all-day meeting, however, involving a fellowship meal, study in depth, and opening and closing worship services. The total amount of time involved is essentially the same as when they met each Sunday, and the members feel it is a more efficient use of time. Perhaps this idea could be put into practice in addition to the regular weekly meetings in some communities.

Already several churches are facing up to the fact that many church members do not regard the church building as the only "holy" ground where worship and study can occur. One creative pastor rides the commuter train into New York once a week with several of his flock in a specially reserved car. The hour on the train is given over to study and discussion. In many communities groups meet in homes for worship and study, and this is the only "church" experience they have. It "counts" the same as Sunday morning.

Regardless, however, of when, where, or in what form worship takes place, it seldom attracts the new breed with a service which is simply a one-man show.

If the pastor is the speaker and those in attendance compose the audience, worship becomes, sadly, a spectator sport, not an experience in which persons participate. The "audience mentality" is the highest barrier that the local church will have to overcome if it is to attract persons who long for genuine participation.

This is perhaps why religious drama, choral presentation, "talk-back" programs, and musical liturgies have so much appeal to the new breed. They offer a chance for each person to be a part of the religious celebration. True, some people undoubtedly would balk at the thought of being so directly involved, but the point is that several on the growing edge of the congregation hunger for more involvement. If a local church is to help set the conditions out of which worship can come, it cannot take for granted which kinds of sermons, sacraments, and worship forms will best set those optimum conditions.

In some local situations, pastors and sensitive laymen may want to support (or even instigate) a kind of "underground" church which would have *no* formal connection with the local congregation. Its "members" would not be on a membership role, and they would not be given pledge cards at the beginning of each church year. They would participate in the program of the church as it involved itself in concerns relevant to their own interests, but probably they would express their concerns through secular media. Their worship would be in small groups, meeting in homes. Hopefully, a few Christians could lead double lives and participate in both churches. This, in some cases, may be the only way that churches can coexist in this interim period of Christian history.

The idea of an underground church is not just a hypothetical one. Christian groups which have no formal connection with established congregations have been started in Rochester, New York, and State College, Pennsylvania. Small groups have been springing up independently in these and other areas, but they share certain characteristics. They meet regularly for worship and discussion. They often develop "disciplines" for study and meditation.

Some of these underground churches, in fact, came to the attention of the news media, and *The National Observer* revealed the following picture:

The Rochester group rents a home to a Negro family displaced by slum clearance. The Cuyahoga Falls "newformers" started a modest human relations class that has spawned an ambitious neighborhood improvement association. Prison visitation is one of several projects of members of the "Sycamore Community" in State College." [2]

Such efforts often encounter resentment, for they are open to the charge that the church is abdicating the responsibility to agitate from within. The local church, through its ministry and concerned laity, may have to work with such groups, however, and encourage them to exist as parallel organizations.

THE REDEMPTIVE COMMUNITY

A second way in which the local church can show its concern for the new breed is to give evidence that the

[2] Lee E. Dirks, "Is the Local Church Out of Date?" Sept. 6, 1965, p. 14.

congregation is taking seriously its responsibilities as a redemptive community. The shortsightedness of some radical Christians is apparent in this area, as the local church *has* worked conscientiously in recent years to *be* a redemptive body. Concerned laymen and ministers have recognized how much shallowness there has been in the so-called religious revival of the fifties and have seen that many local churches, while rich in members, are often poor in *koinonia*.

Christian fellowship, if it is to be taken seriously by the new breed, will have to be manifest in certain ways. Being, or becoming, a redemptive community is almost as difficult to arrange as is setting the conditions for worship. The truly redemptive fellowship is that which is true to the leadership of the Holy Spirit. It has a depth which makes life-change possible. It is more than a "friendly" church, more than an institution with something printed on its stationery as a letterhead, and more than robot-like ushers who smile cheerfully at the door. It is also different from the tight little cliques which many small-town and rural churches mistakenly think is *koinonia*.

The kind of Christian fellowship which will win back Christians disenchanted with the status of the church as it now is, is that which will show it can accept people as they are. Any sociological study which seeks to do so can indicate the status consciousness of the local church. We know that some churches seem to cater to the carriage trade, others to the lower socio-economic groups, and still others to those people who are too poor to be members of the carriage trade and too proud to join the lower socio-economic congregations.

The truly redemptive congregation, so far as the

new breed is concerned, will also demonstrate its openness to people of all races and colors. Obviously, this means the acceptance of people of other races, but it means more than this token policy. It may mean that they will sign resolutions favoring open housing and equal job opportunity. This minimal effort does only a little to help Negroes find homes or jobs, but it is good for a congregation to go on record in such things for its own sake.

It also means that the congregation goes beyond the token Race Relations Sunday observances, which are worth a little to God's kingdom—but not much. Better than these efforts are congregational exchanges, in which half of a white congregation worships with half of a Negro church on given Sundays. It could mean a yearlong exchange of members or even the permanent merging of units within the churches, such as the men's or women's fellowship.

Congregations can demonstrate their sincerity, too, by opening their homes to children from slum areas for summer vacations. They can provide weekend homes for welfare agencies which seek homes for orphan children. One entire congregation learned much about its redemptive purposes because a family within its membership provided, from time to time, a home for unwed girls who were expecting babies. In fact, when individuals like this set the pace, the redemptive quality of an entire congregation is often revealed—for better or worse. This is a living symbol of redemptive concern.

Indeed, we cannot underestimate the importance of the symbolic or personal acts of members within established churches as an effective means of showing that some—perhaps many—within a congregation do have a redemptive concern for people. One Chicago church, the Wellington Avenue Church of Christ, decided to mortgage their church property for $10,000, which was then given to organized efforts in the battle for racial freedom. Twenty of the parishioners attended a dinner at a Black Muslim restaurant on Chicago's south side and discussed black power with Negroes there.

The First Congregational Church of Wilmette had eight families who volunteered to live on a standard welfare allowance and contribute the balance to the poor. In Portland, Oregon, a group of churches started the "Outside In," a drop-in center where runaways can find shelter, food, medical service, and other assistance. The same organization of churches (Hub-Cap) carries on a dynamic program of action involving projects in employment training, rehabilitation of homeless men, communication with single men, and recreation.

Normal Park Methodist Church in Chicago presented a six-hour "Soul Sunday" program in an attempt to expose its members to literature, history, and music from the black experience. Other churches started interracial study groups which watched the remarkable TV series "In Black America" and then discussed its implications for their communities. Efforts such as these do not really do very much to solve the ongoing social problems of our time, but they do lend credence to the claim of Christians that churches can be redemptive communities, congregations of people who care for people—with no strings attached.

The redemptive quality of a congregation is also demonstrated when the church functions as a forum. Indeed, it may be at the point of the willingness—or unwillingness—of local congregations to discuss controversial issues that *koinonia* will live or die. For when the church is a forum, those Christians who regard it as the last bastion of middle-class morality and the custodian of the *status quo* may have to eat their words.

How the forum operates will vary from situation to situation. The ground rules, however, are essentially the same: in the name of a search for God's truth, *any* problem or topic can be discussed and debated. Christians can rejoice in the local church as a place wherein birth control, abortion, the pill, premarital sex, legalized gambling, interracial marriage, the war in Vietnam, the death of God, and the hippies can be discussed. Not only will they be discussed, if there are new breed around, but you can be sure there will be open and frank discussion—and probably considerable disagreement.

Family night discussions could be used. A sermon could be preached on the announced topic with a talkback following the service. Small groups discussing a common problem is another means used by the forum. Calling in "experts" (e.g., a Negro to discuss black power) for special meetings is still another way in which the local church can *be* a forum.

There is more to being a forum, of course, than simply saying that any topic can be discussed. The fact is that most topics will not be discussed, or if they are, they may be discussed in a shallow and meaningless way. The church, if it would attract the new breed back to it, will have to sponsor the forum and insuire genuine dialogue. It may have to do this in both traditional and creative ways. One of the creative ways that this could be done is by sponsoring programs such as "Sunday Night at the Movies!" Good films, supposedly secular, can be shown with planned discussion afterward. Films such as *Nothing But a Man* or *A Time for Burning* or any one of several anti-war films can be shown—and the issues will then raise themselves. *The Parable,* the well-known film which appeared first at the New York World's Fair, plays consistently to standing-room-only crowds on college campuses. Could it not be the means for dialogue between new- and old-breed Christians in a local church?

Finally, the local church can show itself to exist for redemptive purposes by opening its facilities to "outsiders." Interestingly enough, the local church has long been open to *some* outside groups which were respectable, such as the Boy Scouts or American Legion Auxiliary. If it wants to show it cares, however, the local congregation can encourage such groups as Alcoholics Anonymous, Head Start, or ghetto nursery-school groups to use its building. Bible school should almost always be interdenominational and interracial. Perhaps the local chapters of the NAACP or CORE should be invited to use a church's facilities.

There is great risk in this, of course, and there is little question that some members will oppose such policies. The degree of trouble in which a church can find itself has recently been demonstrated by the First Presbyterian Church of Chicago and its pastor, John R. Fry. That church worked with and through the Rangers, a Negro youth gang, in an effort to deal with serious inner-city problems. The minister and the church were accused of many immoral activities, none of which was really substantiated. That church showed itself to be a community which cared for the outcast—the Rangers—regardless of personal cost. It illustrates, to the extreme, what local congregations will have to be if the new breed is to take them seriously.

THE COMMUNITY OF ACTION

It is common to criticize the parish church for its silence on the racial issue, but this silence merely shows considerable color blindness. In the South it has been the local Negro church which has been the center of social witness and concern, and the bombing and burning of these churches are the clearest evidence that they have been very "relevant" indeed. If WASP churches can speak to the problems of white racism in the way that southern Negro churches have taken the lead in confronting injustice to black people, the local church can be a community of action.

This confrontation is more than a matter of talk. It involves more than a discussion of the Kerner Report or consideration of the issues in a forum. It involves WASP congregations, confronting the structures of a community which keep the Negro down and deny him his opportunity. In practical terms congregations can get at the problem of white racism in several ways—if they have the will. Meetings can be arranged with realtors to stimulate more open housing. Petitions of support for local human relations commissions which investigate discrimination can be sponsored. One church had a group within it whose members actually went with Negroes who were looking for houses and apartments, sometimes persuading landlords to rent or sell and, on occasion, buying the property and immediately reselling it to the Negro home-seeker.

Other groups within churches have made private resolutions among themselves to disaffiliate with any private club or organization which practices discrimination. Other congregations have pooled resources to provide low-cost loans to poor people who want better accommodations. Don Stevens, lay leader of a suburban Milwaukee Methodist church, summed up the experience of his church in grappling with white racism:

It becomes increasingly clear that massive individual enlightenment is sorely needed to preclude urban upheaval in the years immediately ahead. The primary chance for success would appear to rest with aggressive young church people, who not only see irrelevance in the church's recent past, but also do not feel the restraint of vested interest.

The Protestant churches, which have within their ranks most of the persons who knowingly, or unknowingly, perpetuate white racism, also have the best opportunity to attack this problem. This the local church, right now, can do.

In dealing with the fruits of white racism—ghettos, illiteracy, poverty, crime, and personal tragedy—local churches probably do better at the present time to complement secular organized efforts than to go off on their own.

One church which has built cooperation with secular agencies into its total church program is the Church of the Saviour (Methodist) in Indianapolis, Indiana. As a regular part of its program and its ongoing work, the members have specific responsibilities—working through a state prison, a settlement house, and in nursing homes. These programs take the place of, or exist in addition to, the usual kind of fellowship-discussion program that most churches have. This church was started with the deliberate intention of achieving certain ends, one of which was the sensible use of time and energy through the agencies best equipped to meet certain needs. Whether or not such a program could be grafted onto an established congregation is another question, but the fact is that this congregation is typical of most suburban congregations in every other way. Certainly, the differences are not as great as they might seem on the surface.

It is reasonable to assume, also, that local established churches could simply make use of the intelligence and ongoing skills of groups such as the League of Women Voters as they seek to develop workable programs of political action. Such groups continually work on crucial and key political ideas, many of which—as any sensible person knows—have obvious religious and moral connotations. Local churches in some areas have taken advantage of the LWV, as well as other political education groups, in arranging for debates between candidates for public offices—debates which center around especially interesting and important religious and moral issues of concern to Christians. These organizations provide information on both sides of an issue, which enables Christians to make relevant moral decisions in the political sphere. They provide avenues through which Christians can work as individuals. In a sense these persons can be "set free" by the church to work for social justice, or an improvement in the welfare system, or in opposition to legalized gambling. Few local churches have the staff or the resources to carry on this struggle by themselves, but in cooperation with secular, political action groups, they can meet the real needs of many members within the congregation who see work in the political sphere as a vital part of Christian witness today.

The reason why working in, through, and with secular agencies will attract the interest of the new-breed Christian is because he, unlike the frustrated idealists of the past, is very much a realist. His realism makes him see that the organizational structure of Christian bodies has become more and more an obstacle to the real work of the church. The mechanical, institutional ways in which local churches carry on their official activities can interfere, he feels, with the free and full functioning of the body of Christ. Its working with secular agencies to serve humanity and the world will be evidence to which we can point that the church institution is not seeking to maintain *itself,* to promote *itself,* to establish *itself.* Being realists, Christians—especially if they engage in dialogue with the established church—will come to see that some kind of institution is a sociological and theological necessity, and they will become able to be at least *loyal* rebels while remaining critical of the *modus operandi* of the church.

Not only can local churches cooperate with secular agencies, they can learn from them. It is very difficult for many Christians, who have carried throughout their families set ideals of the church and an exclusive view of its work in the world, to recognize the fact that local congregations have a great deal to learn from secular agencies. Yet where churches have taken this fact seriously, they have been able to restructure their programs so as to illustrate that established congregations can serve sufficiently and effectively in their local communities. Only six years ago Broadway Methodist Church in Indianapolis was called a cathedral with the largest congregation of its denomination in the state. When the first Negro family moved into the community, the congregation was shaken to its foundations. Some of the congregation moved away and sold their homes, but because they "loved Broadway Methodist Church," they promised to keep coming there. As the population became more and more Negro—it reached 70 percent in a few years—James Armstrong, the pastor (now a bishop), and some laymen who had his kind of courage, led a struggle to modify the program of that church to enable it to meet the needs of its community.

Instead of moving to the suburbs, the church, which had been known for its wealth, remained and became known for its service. They sponsored a weekday program which included recreational programs for three hundred youngsters, mostly Negroes, under the guidance of a former college boxing champion, an ex-professional football player, and a judo-karate instructor. They sponsored afternoon tutoring sessions for slow readers, youngsters who would be dropouts had not such a program been put in operation. They opened a thrift shop which offers good used clothing at a small cost. They sponsored a health center directed by a former medical missionary, who persuaded other medical doctors and nurses to cooperate in providing prenatal care and planned-parenthood clinics.

This kind of program has been started by a few churches in the inner city, which illustrates the fact that established congregations, faced with the needs of a community, can stay and meet them if they can psychologically change their attitudes. In fact, the real problem is not so much in finding the techniques and the skills and the personnel to head up such programs; the real problem is in facing the psychological attitudes of rigidity and inflexibility that plague so many of our churches. New-breed Christians can offer this psychological courage which established congregations need. Established congregations many times have excellent contacts and effective ways of accomplishing the ends that are sought—if they can have their attitudes confronted by the challenge of using secular agencies and secular ideas for the service of the Christian God. The churches which are not so large or influential as Broadway Methodist Church can be, hopefully, catalytic agents within secular agencies which can deal with human problems. The main point is that the needs be met, not *who* meets them.

Local churches are more helpless in the area of peace than in the area of race relations. Discussing the issues frankly, as mentioned earlier, is certainly progress, although this seems too little to many Christians. Churches may also have to raise the fact of alternative service with their young people, if they expect these young people to become adults who take seriously the threat of war in the world. Can local churches suggest and endorse registration for conscientious objection and a 1-O classification? Can churches encourage their youth to enlist in the Peace Corps and VISTA? Can study groups be formed to consider the biblical base of peace? The new breed is not composed primarily of persons from the so-called peace chuches, and now, in a new way, the questions of peace and the military establishment are live issues.

Traditional churches with traditional programs have a realistic place in today's world. They clearly are speaking to the needs of some by virtue of the fact that they are surviving and even prospering. They are not as reactionary as the new breed may think, nor are they as close-minded as some of their outspoken leaders would lead others to think. Almost all local churches could profit from the freshness (in both senses) of the new breed, and certainly, many radical Christians are looking and longing for a base for expressing deeply felt and life-changing concerns.

In a world full of problems and temptations, with wolves disguished as sheep and, in the minds of some, devils dressed in angels' robes, we cannot afford the luxury of religious infighting. The revolution has come, and the only realistic choice Christians have is between an orderly dialogue in which the necessary sorting and sifting can take place, or the self-righteous sniping and carping which is now going on. The test is a crucial one, for it confronts us all where it hurts the most—at the point of our pet ideas, long-standing beliefs, and personal self-images. It asks us whether we are willing to lose ourselves in the search for the living God. This is not a new question, of course, and the hard fact is that the answer will cost us considerable pain and soul-searching. The only thing worse, though, is not to have asked the question at all.

QUESTIONS FOR DISCUSSION

1. Are there any "sacred forms" which we cannot change and still expect *Christian worship* to take place? For example, would you object to using, instead of the traditional cross, a picture of a black Jesus hanging from a tree? What would be lost? What would be gained? Would you object to a communion service using coffee and doughnuts as the elements? What suggestions do you have for effective symbols and sacraments? Do we simply need better education about the ones we have?

2. Do you think church members and ministers should identify with or even instigate "underground churches"? Does this seem devisive to you? Does it handicap the very dialogue between the "old" and the "new" breeds that this book is promoting?

3. How do you respond to the author's suggestion that lengthy exchanges with Negro churches could be made? Is this only tokenism? To the invitation to slum children to visit our communities (and our churches) on vacation?

4. Consider this situation: One of the crew members of the ship *Phoenix,* which carried medical supplies to North Vietnam, is available to speak to your church group. Should he be allowed to come? What if the larger community objects?

5. Do you agree that the most effective way local churches can act is by confronting "white racism"? What good does signing open-housing ordinances or making church resolutions do? Would you be willing to help a Negro find an apartment to rent?

6. Please indicate by checking the appropriate column whether the church should involve itself in the issues described below. Be prepared to discuss the issues in the following terms: (A) whether you think the issue is ap-

propriate or inappropriate for church groups to consider and (B) if appropriate, whether the particular *way* of handling it or presenting it is proper.

Approve   Disapprove

(1) The chairman of the Social Action Committee has asked the church to pay an attorney, who will be hired to fight the granting of a liquor license to a local hotel.

(2) You have been asked to travel with the members of your church group to the state legislature to lobby against capital punishment, the repeal of which is before the lawmakers.

(3) Your minister has asked the official board of your church *to pass a resolution* favoring open housing in your community, regardless of race, creed, or color.

(4) The Women's Society of your church is debating whether it should circulate a petition *opposing* a bill which would stop Aid-to-Dependent-Children p a y - ments for women on welfare after the third child.

(5) Your minister has just preached a sermon opposing America's escalation of the war in Vietnam.

Approve   Disapprove

(6) Your denomination has sent out a letter urging its members to write their congressmen and express their opposition to a bill which would remove the tax-exempt status of churches.

(7) Your adult Sunday school class has been asked to lobby at the state legislature against pari-mutuel betting.

(8) An *ad hoc* committee from your church has asked you to sign a petition favoring a bill advocating Sunday closing for businesses, which will be sent to your representative.

(9) Your official board has been asked to endorse a bill raising the minimum wage to $1.50 per hour.

(10) An all-church meeting is being held to decide whether or not your congregation should endorse a Reform Republican who is running for Councilman from your district.

(11) You have been asked to go to Washington to visit congressmen for the purpose of lobbying against a draft lottery. It has been suggested that your travel expenses

119

Approve   Disapprove

might be taken out of the Social Action Committee's budget.

(12) The Mental Health Association has asked your church to petition the governor to restore funds for salary increases for the state mental hospital staff which had recently been cut from the state budget.

7. What practical ways do you see in which you as a Christial could use your position and resources to help fight poverty and racism?

8. Where do we go from here?

BIBLIOGRAPHY

Barr, Browne. *Parish Back Talk*. Nashville: Abingdon Press, 1964.

Cate, William B. *The Ecumenical Scandal on Main Street*. New York: Association Press, 1965.

Clark, M. Edward, William L. Malcomson, and Warren L. Molton, eds. *The Church Creative*. Nashville: Abingdon Press. 1967.

Fisher, Wallace. *From Tradition to Mission*. Nashville: Abingdon Press, 1965.

Jud, Gerald J. *Pilgrim's Process*. Philadelphia: Pilgrim Press, 1967.

Judy, Marvin T. *The Cooperative Parish in Nonmetropolitan Areas*. Nashville: Abingdon Press, 1967.

Raines, Robert A. *Reshaping the Christian Life.* New York: Harper & Row, 1964.

Report of the National Advisory Commission on Civil Disorders. New York: Bantam Books, 1968.

Schaller, Lyle E. *The Local Church Looks to the Future.* Nashville: Abingdon Press, 1968.

Younger, George D. *The Church and Urban Power Structure.* Philadelphia: Westminster Press, 1963.

index

123

Date Due

DE 19'80			

Demco 38-297